I would, but
MY DAMN MIND
won't let me!

I would, but MY DAMN MIND won't let me!

A Young Man's Guide to
Understanding His Thoughts and Feelings

Words of Wisdom for Young Men

Book 1

Jacqui Letran

Joseph Wolfgram

PORT ISABEL, TEXAS

First edition: © December 2022 by Jacqui Letran and Joseph Wolfgram.

This book is licensed for your personal enjoyment and education only. Nothing in this book should be construed as personal advice or diagnosis, and the suggestions found herein must not be used in this manner. The information in this book should not be considered as complete and does not cover all diseases, ailments, physical conditions, or their treatment. You should consult with your physician regarding the applicability of any information provided herein and before beginning any exercise, weight-loss, or health-care program.

All rights reserved. No part of this publication may be reproduced, distributed, or transmitted in any form or by any means, including photocopying, recording, or other electronic or mechanical methods, without the prior written permission of the publisher, except in the case of brief quotations embodied in critical reviews and certain other noncommercial uses permitted by copyright law.

Publisher's Cataloging-In-Publication Data

Names: Letran, Jacqui. Wolfgram, Joseph.
Title: I would, but my damn mind won't let me: a young man's guide to understanding his thoughts and feelings/ Jacqui Letran, Joseph Wolfgram.
Description: 1st edition. | Port Isabel, Texas: A Healed Mind [2022] | Series: Words of wisdom for young men series | Interest age level: 12 and up.
Identifiers: ISBN 978-1-952719-17-2 (hardcover) | ISBN 978-1-952719-16-5 (paperback)
Subjects: LCSH: Adolescent psychology. | Teenagers--Attitudes. | Happiness in adolescence. | Emotions in adolescence. | Self-help techniques for teenagers.
Classification: LCC BF724.L48 2022 (print) | LCC BF724 (e-book) | DDC 155.5--dc2

Table of Contents

Why Can't You Just Control Yourself? 1
    60-Second Reader 5
    Self-Reflection 6

Your Conscious vs. Your Subconscious Mind 9
    60-Second Reader 26

The Belief System 31
    60-Second Reader 41

The Stranger Danger Protocol 45
    60-Second Reader 57

Case Studies 61

I'm Not Good Enough 63
    Self-Reflection 75

I'm Not Worthy 77
    Self-Reflection 90

I'm Not Loved 93
    Self-Reflection 105

I'm Not Safe 107
    Self-Reflection 118

A Powerful Beginning 121
About the Authors 123
With Gratitude 125
Connect with Us 126

Words of Wisdom for Teens Series Award-Winning Guides for Teen Girls 127

Stop the Bully Within Podcast 128

Dedication

This book is dedicated to all the young men out there who are struggling with low confidence, self-doubt, or self-sabotaging thoughts and actions. Even though you may not believe it yet, we know that you have everything you need within yourself to overcome your struggles. We believe in you. We know that you can make significant positive changes in your life by understanding and commanding your mind. Read this book with an open mind and a willingness to try something different. Get ready to be amazed by the results you'll find.

CHAPTER 1

Why Can't You Just Control Yourself?

How many times have you been told by well-meaning parents, other adults, or even your friends that you should just stop thinking, feeling, or acting a certain way? They tell you that the problems you have are all in your head. They tell you to stop making a big deal out of things, that you're too high-strung, and there is no reason to be upset.

And yet, you are. You don't know what to think or how to feel. You feel tense and nervous. You have emotions that you do not understand. And when you look around, others seem to have it so easy. But for you, life is difficult and unfair!

Your situation may seem hopeless; perhaps you have even decided that you were just "born that way" and there is nothing you can do to change.

But what if you are wrong about that conclusion? What if there is a way for you to create the changes you want to see in your life? What if we can teach you how to take control of your thoughts, feelings, and actions? Would you want to learn how to do that for yourself?

The power of the human mind is incredible. It is much more powerful than you've been taught. In fact, most people don't know this, so they can't teach you how to use your mind to your benefit.

Your mind is capable of creating horrible life experiences, where every day is filled with negative, stressful, and depressing moments. The mind is also capable of creating happy, successful, and enjoyable moments for you to experience as well. It might not feel that way right now, but you are the only one who gets to choose which type of life experiences you'll have—no matter what is happening around you!

Once you learn easy, yet highly effective ways to take charge of your mind, you'll find that you have the power to create the life you want and deserve. The power to create permanent, positive change is available to you, even if it feels as if your struggles are overwhelming right now.

You can stop wasting your energy and time on those old, useless thoughts and feelings. Today is the day to change your life experiences for good.

This book will show you how to:
- Challenge your old, negative belief patterns.
- Stop unhealthy thoughts and feelings.
- Create positive life experiences for yourself.
- Stay calm and in control in any situation.

Everyone's journey to happiness begins with the belief that happiness is possible. Even if your past experiences have led you to believe you will have a difficult life, filled with stress, anxiety, and unhappiness, we will show you that you do have other options. You can learn to create the happiness you deserve.

In this book, we will teach you how to take charge of your mind to overcome obstacles, breeze through challenges, and create a great life for yourself. We show you simple, yet powerful principles to strengthen your self-belief and help you establish a solid foundation for success and happiness.

The next time somebody asks you, "Why can't you just control yourself?" you can smile and thank them for the gentle reminder and instantly take control of your thoughts and feelings again.

You already have the key to your success and happiness, and we are going to show you how to use it.

Close your eyes now for just a moment and imagine how wonderful your life will be once you fully understand how to manage your thoughts, feelings, and actions. You can be someone who has it all under control, projecting confidence and success. You can make decisions quickly with confidence. You can be the person others aspire to be.

So read this book with an open mind and a willingness to try something new for the results you deserve. We can't promise that life will always be easy, but we can show you how to be in control and remain positive and productive, rising above the challenges to enjoy a life worth living every day!

Get ready to be impressed by how quickly you can take charge of your life now.

60-Second Reader

1. You get to choose your life experiences.
2. You have the power to create the life you want and deserve.
3. The power to create permanent, positive change is available to you, even with your current struggles.
4. You can learn to:
   - Challenge your old, negative beliefs and thought patterns.
   - Stop unhealthy thoughts and feelings.
   - Create positive life experiences for yourself.
   - Stay calm and in control in any situation.
   - Unleash the power of your mind to create the life you want and deserve.
   - Be happy.

Self-Reflection

Take five minutes to think about how your life will be once you can stop those negative thoughts from occurring and, instead, focus on the positive points of every situation. What would that look like? What would you do? How would your life be different?

Use your imagination and have fun with this self-reflection. Write down all the great things you'll finally be able to do. Remember to think and dream big!

Example 1: Make a list of goals.
1. Speaking confidently in all situations.
2. Making friends easily.
3. Being confident, courageous, and outgoing
4. Taking on new challenges with enthusiasm.
5. Becoming an undefeated tennis player for my school district.
6. Inspiring people to come to me for advice.
7. Becoming the valedictorian for my class.

Example 2: Write a short story
I am proud of who I am and what I am capable of. I go after what I want with confidence and enthusiasm. I let go of stuff easily and stay positive even when things are challenging. I am outgoing and make friends easily. I am welcomed and accepted wherever I go. I am smart and talented. I am happy and successful. Life is good!

8 | I WOULD, BUT MY DAMN MIND WON'T LET ME!

CHAPTER 2

Your Conscious vs. Your Subconscious Mind

To take control of your mind, it is important to understand the differences between the conscious mind and the subconscious mind and the roles that each part plays in your life.

Your Conscious Mind

The conscious part of your mind is your logical self. It can process events from your past, present, and future. It solves problems and stores your goals and dreams. It has free will to reject or accept concepts and ideas.

There are three main things to know and remember about your conscious mind:

1. It's responsible for logic, reasoning, and decision-making.

2. It controls all your intentional actions.
3. It acts as a filtering system, rejecting or accepting information.

What Does This Mean?

The conscious part of your mind is the part that you are aware of. It's the part of your mind that you use when you are learning a new concept. For example, it helps you to learn how to ride a bike. When you are in the learning phase, you are consciously focused on how to balance yourself, how to pedal, and how to maneuver without crashing into something or losing your balance. All those thoughts and actions are the work of your conscious mind—something you are fully aware of.

Your conscious mind is also responsible for collecting data, processing the data, and making decisions based on the information at hand. It is the part of your mind that makes simple decisions, such as "I want to wear my black jacket because it will protect me from the rain." It also makes more complicated decisions, such as which college to apply to, based on the career path you want to follow.

While your conscious mind is amazing in its ability to collect, process, and make sense of data, it has limitations. Did you know that your conscious mind can only process less than one percent of all the data available to you at any moment?

*COOL FACT: At any given time, you can only consciously focus on **less than one percent** of all the things that are going on within yourself and your environment.*

Even if you could process ten times this amount, you would still be missing ninety percent of the information and data available. That's a very incomplete picture.

Knowing this should cause you to ask some questions about your life experiences so far: "What have I been missing? What information did I not even detect? How would my life improve if I changed which information I focused on?"

Later, we will explain this concept and show you how to use this knowledge to take control of your thoughts and actions so you can take control of your life. Before we dive into that, let's talk about your subconscious mind and its functions.

Your Subconscious Mind

Your subconscious mind reacts based on instincts, habits, and learning from past experiences that are programmed into what we call your "Master Plan."

The Master Plan is a detailed set of instructions (like a movie script) that tells your subconscious mind what to do. Your subconscious mind does not have free will. Any ideas, thoughts, or feelings that get into the subconscious part of your mind stay there.

There are five main things to know and remember about your subconscious mind:
1. It is responsible for all your involuntary actions (breathing, heart beating, etc.).
2. It is one hundred percent automatic and follows scripts (a pre-programmed set of instructions); it has no ideas or thoughts of its own.
3. It stores ALL your memories, life experiences, learned information, and beliefs.
4. Its main function is to keep you alive and "safe."
5. Your subconscious mind processes information visually—through pictures and images (called an "Internal Representation," or "IR" for short).

COOL FACT: The subconscious mind is that part of your mind that is NOT within your awareness. It works quietly behind the scenes, tucked away in a dark corner, so you won't really notice it or its activities.

Unlike the conscious part of your mind, which can only focus on one percent of the available data, your subconscious mind can process one hundred percent of every bit of data it encounters, every second! That's right… your subconscious mind is one hundred percent aware of everything that's happening within you and around you, every single second of every single day.

The Master Plan

When you were born, you arrived with a "pre-programmed" Master Plan, which is a detailed set of instructions and algorithms that tells your subconscious mind what to do. In your infancy and early years, that Master Plan includes only basic, yet very important instructions that tell your subconscious mind what to do to keep you alive—such as breathing, regulating your heartbeat, or digesting food.

This Master Plan also has information handed down from your parents and ancestors in the form of genetics, such as your hair and eye color.

However, you were not born with a Master Plan for your belief system, your core values, or the things you will learn in the future. The information you use to create the majority of your Master Plan is given to you during the first seven years of your life by the people closest to you, and through your own life experiences.

Your Master Plan is ever-changing, a constant work in progress. It is always adapting and evolving, influenced by your current situation and the objectives you have chosen for yourself.

Your conscious mind is responsible for adding to the Master Plan based on your life experiences. In a future chapter, we will discuss how your conscious mind programs the Master Plan. For right now, just know that you have a Master Plan from which your subconscious mind is always operating.

Your Subconscious Mind Simplified

To simplify the concept and help you understand the power of your mind, think of your subconscious mind as a room full of movies—a personal movie library of your very own. In this library, there are thousands (or even millions!) of movies of you and your life experiences.

Within this movie library, there is a recording device and a Movie Operator. Your Movie Operator's job is to follow the Master Plan, which, again, is a pre-programmed set of detailed instructions provided by your conscious mind. In this way, your conscious mind behaves like the writer and director, and your subconscious mind is the actor carrying out the directions within the scripts.

The recording device within your subconscious mind is always "on" and actively recording everything you are experiencing, every second of every day. Every one of your experiences EVER—whether it's a thought, a feeling, or an action—is recorded in your movies.

Using the instructions in your Master Plan, your Movie Operator labels, sorts, and stores your movies into your subconscious mind's library. That Master Plan also tells your Movie Operator when to add or remove a movie from your "favorite playlist" and when to play a movie back to you.

Besides recording, sorting, storing, and playing your movies, your Movie Operator has a bigger job. That job is to protect you and keep you safe from any real or perceived danger. Likewise, your conscious mind has an important duty—that is, to create a Master Plan of what to do in any given situation. That's a massive job, but the only tools your subconscious mind has are the movies it has recorded of you and the instructions within the Master Plan.

Who's the Boss?

Given the information presented so far, who do you think is the boss—your conscious mind or your subconscious mind?

If you guessed your conscious mind, you are correct! Your conscious mind is always the boss. It's the part of your mind capable of processing and analyzing data. It's the part of your mind that has free will to make decisions and can accept or reject information. It's the part of your mind that selects the information to incorporate into your Master Plan.

Your Reality Exists Only in Your Mind

Do you remember when we said your conscious mind can only process less than one percent of the data you encounter, while your subconscious mind can process one hundred percent? What does that mean?

To put things into perspective, your subconscious mind receives millions of bits of data every single second. Millions of bits of data every single second! Stop and take that in for a moment. Every single second of your life, your subconscious mind is bombarded by millions of bits of data, which is equivalent to all the words in seven volumes of average-sized books. That's a lot of information to process every single second.

Imagine what it would be like for you if you were aware of millions of bits of data every single second of your life. How would you feel if you were forced to process seven volumes every single second? Your conscious mind is just not capable of processing that much data. You would be overloaded with information and would most likely explode or shut down. Luckily for you, all of that is happening in the background of your subconscious mind and is not within your awareness.

Of the millions of bits of data, the conscious part of your mind can only process 126 bits of data per second. To show what this looks like, let's consider the example of the millions of bits of data as being equivalent to all the words within seven volumes. Of the seven books that your subconscious mind is processing, your conscious mind can only see one word. One word! That one word, whichever one word that might be, is the only one that makes it into your awareness and ultimately becomes your reality.

Stop for a moment and think about what that means. Imagine understanding only one word while reading seven entire books and believing that all seven books are about just that single word. Is there something you might be missing?

The important takeaway here is to realize that each of us is most likely focusing on a different word, and that becomes our unique reality.

> ***COOL FACT:*** *Your reality only exists in your mind and nowhere else. You might be in the same situation with other people but can have a completely different experience!*

Try this exercise out for fun. Close your eyes and turn to a random page in this book and point to a word. Now, open your eyes and look at that word. Does this one word represent everything this book is about?

We can guarantee that the answer is *no*. This book is about much more than the one word you've randomly selected, but it's a good illustration of how your mind creates your experience in each moment by filtering out a ton of information.

> ***COOL FACT:*** *You have the power to create a new and better reality for yourself by choosing to focus on positive aspects in every moment!*

The Importance Center

How does your mind decide which one word, out of the seven volumes, to focus your attention on? Within your mind, you have a part called the Reticular Activating System. The Reticular Activating System is responsible for many functions. In this book, we will focus on its role in creating your reality. We like to refer to the

Reticular Activating System as the "Importance Center," or "IC" for short. (To help you remember this, think of the IC as "I see" and recall that the IC determines the experience you get to have, out of everything happening around you!)

Remember when we mentioned the Master Plan before? The Master Plan is kept here in the IC and tells your subconscious mind which information to send to your conscious mind.

All your significant information is stored here—your belief system, your values, your significant emotional experiences, and your key learning situations.

> **COOL FACT:** *Your Importance Center is as unique as your fingerprint. No two people have the exact same IC. That's why you can be at the same event as someone else and have a completely different experience.*

From the millions of bits of data it receives, your subconscious mind filters them through the IC. If it finds something that resembles the contents of your IC, that information gets pushed to your conscious awareness. If there is no similarity, your subconscious mind will either dismiss it, generalize it, or distort it to make it "fit" within your Master Plan.

Let's say your dad buys a brand-new car—a white Tesla Model 3. Soon after, you begin to see the same vehicle in the same color everywhere you go. Have bunches of people suddenly bought the same car?

No. Most likely, those cars have been on the road all along, but it wasn't an important detail for you until your dad bought that car. Once your dad bought the Tesla Model 3, it entered your IC, which tells your subconscious mind to focus your attention every time it sees a car of the same make and color.

You might be hyper-aware of all the white Tesla Model 3s for a while, but once the car becomes old news, you will stop seeing it as frequently. Does this mean that tons of people have sold their cars, and they are now off the road? No. All it means is that, at this moment in your life, that car is no longer importance, so it doesn't get pushed to your conscious awareness at every sighting.

It's important to note that the IC has short-term and long-term parameters, or instructions, that it's following. Short-term parameters are things that might be important to you right now, for a brief time—like what's in style currently, or the newness of a song. It could be a few days, a few weeks, or even months from now, but short-term parameters have an end date.

Long-term parameters stay with you for extended periods of time. Often, they remain with you permanently unless you purposefully remove them. Long-term parameters can be as simple as learned activities, such as riding your bike, or more complex, such as your belief system, values, attitudes, or reactions to different events.

Have you noticed how people can respond very differently to the same events? This is because the parameters in their ICs are different. Knowing this should help you understand that you get to decide for yourself how to respond and react in every situation.

You get to choose to respond in a way that brings you happiness and success, rather than allowing your old programs to control you.

The Personal Assistant You Didn't Know You Have

How would you like to have a personal assistant who is there for you 24/7? How amazing would it be to have not only such an assistant, but one who eagerly awaits your every command and obeys those commands without questioning you? That sounds cool, right?

What if we told you that you do have that personal assistant already, but you have been giving your assistant some rather poor commands? Commands that are getting you the results you are experiencing right now. Results that you may no longer want, or even dread getting. Would you like to learn more about your assistant and, more importantly, how to command your assistant to create the better results that you want?

You might have guessed by now that your subconscious mind is your personal assistant. Your subconscious mind's job is to create whatever experience you requested in the best way possible.

What you might not know is that every thought you have and every emotion you feel is a command to your subconscious mind to give you more of the same.

That's right. Every thought you have and every emotion you feel is a command to your subconscious mind: "This is the experience I want. Give me more!"

If you said, "I'm so stressed," your subconscious mind understands that as a command: "I want to be stressed. Look for evidence to support why I should be stressed. Give me more reasons to feel stressed."

Once you give that command, your subconscious mind will load that into your IC and immediately look for stressful details in your environment. Details that could stress you out get pushed to your awareness. In addition, your subconscious mind will scan your movie library to find stressful movies from your past and play them in the background for you.

You are the boss. When you ask for stress, your subconscious mind goes to work to create that experience for you automatically and without delay!

Does this sound familiar? How many times have you felt stressed about something, then started having stressful thoughts about something else? Soon, you became overwhelmed with stress and other negative feelings. This is because whatever you focus on, you're telling your mind, "This is the experience I want. Give me more of this!"

> **COOL FACT:** *Whatever you are focusing on, you are telling your subconscious mind to give you more of that thing. It's like feeding a monster food and watching it grow out of control right in front of your eyes!*

The good news is that the process works both ways. This means that when you focus on something positive, that positive thing will also grow. If you are stressed out, you can decide to focus on being calm instead, and watch your reality shift to something new and better.

Staying Calm Under Stress

You have an assistant who will obey your every command, so use your assistant to your benefit. In stressful moments, you can say to yourself, "Even though I feel stressed, I choose to be calm."

Say, "I choose to be calm" several times to catch your assistant's attention. Once that occurs, start repeating, "I am calm. I am calm. I am calm." As you repeat, "I am calm," imagine yourself doing something that calms you down. It might be reading a book, walking on the beach, or playing your favorite music.

With these "choosing calm" steps, you are telling your assistant, "Even though I am stressed, I choose to be calm. Calm looks like this. This is the experience I want. Give me more of this." Such a clear instruction makes it simple for your subconscious mind to bring you back to a state of calmness.

Regardless of what negative emotion you experience, we recommend that you give your assistant the command, "I choose to be calm. I am calm." Calmness is a wonderful place to be. Being calm is like a reset; it tells your assistant to stop playing the old negative movies, so you have a blank screen. From a place of calmness, it is easier to look at the current situation for what it is, decide what you want, and take the actions that best suit your needs.

COOL FACT: Whether you focus on the negative or the positive aspects of any event, you must spend energy on those thoughts. Why not focus your energy on positive, powerful thoughts that will create the results you're looking for?

What Does Google Have to Do With Your Mind?

Here's another important detail to help you command your subconscious mind effectively. Your subconscious mind is like a Google search engine. When you type something into the search bar and press *enter*, you'll get results that match that search request.

Just like the Google search engine, your subconscious mind cannot process negative commands. When you give your subconscious mind a negative command, it will ignore the negative part of it and focus on the remaining part of the command.

This is because of the Internal Representation (or IR) that we mentioned earlier in this chapter, when discussing the subconscious mind.

Remember when we said that your subconscious mind processes information by creating pictures and movies? When we tell you, "Think of spilling milk," what picture comes to mind for you? That is how your subconscious mind understands those words.

If we say, "Don't spill the milk," what picture comes to mind? The picture you visualize is not "don't spill the milk." That's because there is no such picture. What might pop up instead is a picture of you holding on to a cup or glass of milk carefully, or a picture of you putting a lid on the cup, or something similar. Those are not pictures of "don't spill the milk." Your subconscious mind, like the Google search engine, cannot process negatives. It cannot make an IR of a "don't," a "not" or even a "no longer."

With Google, if you type into the search bar, "Don't find me blue cars," and press *enter*, Google's search return will include tons of things related to blue cars. It completely ignores the "don't" part.

Try it out for yourself. Do a Google search using "don't" and see what results you'll get. Better yet, let's do a simple experiment right now. Ready? Here it is. Our command to you is, "Don't think of an orange elephant."

What happened? The first thing you thought of was an orange elephant, wasn't it? When you realized you were thinking of an orange elephant, you might have tried to force yourself to imagine the elephant in another color or think of something else entirely different. That's interesting, isn't it?

You should be having some "aha" moments right now. Think back over the past week or two and consider what commands you have given to your subconscious mind that are causing you to have some of your negative feelings and experiences.

Now that you are aware of how your subconscious mind interprets instructions, pay attention to the thoughts you're thinking and the feelings you're feeling. If the thoughts or feelings are negative, you can choose differently. This is where the "I choose to be calm" instruction comes in handy. That command lets your assistant know you have chosen to be calm instead of upset, stressed, or whatever you are experiencing.

> **COOL FACT**: *You are the boss, and your subconscious mind is your assistant. If you catch yourself giving your subconscious mind a negative thought or a bad command, do something about it. Your assistant will carry out whatever command you provide unless you consciously revise it.*

Let's say your mom is making dinner. She asks if you would rather have pizza or tacos. You say "pizza" but immediately change your mind to tacos. When you realize this, chances are you correct yourself and tell your mom you want tacos. I doubt that you would just sit there and expecting your mom to read your mind and prepare tacos instead.

You can do the same thing with your subconscious mind. Let's say you think, "I'm too angry to focus now," and you catch yourself thinking that. Rather than just letting it go, you can say, "Uh, I mean, I'm willing to focus." Or you can say, "Erase that" or "Delete that," or use similar phrases to tell your subconscious mind what you want to do with the misinformation. You can also say, "I'm in control of myself and I choose to focus on…"

The "I choose to be calm" command works well here, too. Commands like these are very powerful because they tell your subconscious mind exactly what you want.

60-Second Reader

1. Your conscious mind is your logical mind that learns, thinks, and decides.
    a. You use this part of your mind to focus on details and become aware of things.
    b. You can only consciously focus on one percent of what's happening inside of you and around you at any given moment.
2. Your subconscious mind is like a program, running automatically in the background of your mind.
    a. You do not have an awareness of, nor can you focus on, the automatic programs of your subconscious mind.
    b. Your subconscious mind can process one hundred percent of everything happening inside and immediately around you.
3. Your "Importance Center," or "IC," contains the automatic programs of your subconscious mind.
    a. Your beliefs and other significant information are stored in your IC.
    b. Your subconscious mind is programmed to look for evidence to support whatever is in your IC.
    c. Your IC is unique to you. No one else has the exact same IC as you, which also means no one else experiences life the way you do.

4. Your subconscious mind is your personal assistant, and you are the boss.
    a. It's programmed to give you the experiences you ask for in the easiest, quickest way possible.
    b. Problem: Every thought you have and emotion you feel is a command to your subconscious mind, "This is what I want; give me more!"
5. Your mind is like a Google search engine. It cannot process negative commands.
    a. When you give a negative command, such as "Don't be angry," your subconscious mind will ignore the "don't" and carry out the rest of the command.
    b. Solution: Give your mind clear, positive commands for what you truly want. Instead of saying, "I don't want to be angry," say, "I choose to be calm."

Notes

Notes

CHAPTER 3

The Belief System

Belief:
1. An acceptance that a statement is true, or that something exists.
2. Something one accepts as true or real; a firmly held opinion or conviction.

Did you know that much of your belief system was developed by the time you were seven years old? Did you also know that much of your belief system was not decided by you but that, in fact, your beliefs were given to you by someone else?

We want you to stop and let that sink in for a bit. Most of your beliefs about who you are and the world around you were "programmed" inside your brain before you turned eight years old!

Why do belief systems get created so early in life? During this part of your growth and development, your subconscious mind is fully formed and operational.

However, your conscious mind, the logical part of your mind, is just beginning to form and is not fully developed yet. A young brain doesn't have a working prefrontal cortex, or the part of your mind that processes logic and makes decisions. Therefore, little kids believe in everything they see or hear. The Easter Bunny, Santa Claus, and the Tooth Fairy are all one hundred percent real to your younger self because your conscious mind is not developed enough to reason and determine, "No, that cannot be true."

The Creation of Beliefs

These are the most common ways for you to develop a new belief:
1. Evidence: This is a rational decision based on cause and effect. For example, every time you break curfew, you get grounded. You will create a belief that breaking curfew results in being grounded.
2. Tradition: This is based on your family and cultural values. For example, if you're raised in a Catholic family, your belief system will likely include many aspects of Catholic teachings.
3. Authority: This is based on what the people in respected roles teach you or tell you about something. An example would be your doctor diagnosing you with depression; therefore, you believe you have depression.

4. Association: This is based on the people you interact with. For example, if you belong to a Mensa club and interact with a bunch of intellectuals, you might believe that intelligence is valued.
5. Revelation: This is based on your gut feelings, insights, and intuitions. For example, sometimes you just have a gut feeling of "I don't trust this person," although you might not know why.

Your subconscious mind records one hundred percent of everything, but that doesn't mean everything you experience becomes part of your belief system. In the beginning, when you do not have a Master Plan for new ideas or a belief system, your subconscious mind just records your events. It doesn't have a label for those events yet, or a way to sort and categorize them.

Everything your subconscious mind records at this point is stored in a "general" category. In fact, in your mind's movie library are many categories of beliefs, similar to "genres" or "types" of movies. The four main movie types are:
1. Instructional: These are things you've learned to do, such as riding a bike or playing a guitar.
2. Factual: These are things you've learned and accepted as truth, like the names of different colors or your date of birth.
3. Emotional: These are the experiences you've had and what the experiences mean to you.
4. General: This is where all the miscellaneous movies are stored.

Let's look closely at how an instructional type of movie might get created. Imagine you are an eight-month-old infant learning how to use a spoon. If you have seen a baby learning to eat with utensils, you know how messy that process is. Often, the baby shovels food onto his chin and cheeks or drops it onto himself completely. That is because there is no instructional tape in his subconscious mind's library that tells him how to feed himself properly yet.

The first time you tried to feed yourself, your subconscious mind recorded the event and stored that movie in the general category of your movie library. The second time you attempted to feed yourself, your subconscious mind recorded it and stored it in the general category again. The third time you tried to feed yourself, your conscious mind might have recognized the same data pattern and told your subconscious mind to sort and store these experiences together.

Once you fully understand how to use a spoon to feed yourself, it becomes an instructional video for "Feeding Self with a Spoon." The next time you go to feed yourself, your subconscious mind replays that movie in the background, and you feed yourself easily without even thinking about it.

Consciously, a lot of things happened simultaneously for your subconscious mind to sort and categorize that movie. Perhaps your mom said, "Let's learn how to use a spoon today," or something similar, every time she handed you a spoon. With repetition, you consciously learned that whenever your mom said, "Let's learn how to use a spoon today," and handed you an object, that object was called a spoon, and it was used to put food into your mouth. You then used this information to create your instructional video.

A major belief is created similarly, either through one significant emotional event, or repetitions of several low-intensity emotional events that happen over time.

Significant Emotional Events

Imagine that you are three years old and you're playing in your room. Like most three-year-olds, you are making a huge mess, throwing toys around, and having a great time. Your mom comes into the room, sees the mess, and gets furious with you. She might force you to quit playing and clean your room. She might yell at you or, if you're in an abusive situation, might hit you or react with some other unwelcome action.

This is certainly a significant emotional event for your three-year-old self. You were just having fun in your room when suddenly your mom grabbed your toys away, hit you on the back of your head, and yelled, "You're a bad boy. Clean up your room now!" You don't have a full understanding of what just happened. All you know is that your fun ended, your mom is angry, and you are in pain. Because this event was so traumatic and the pain was significant, your conscious mind immediately accepts the situation as a fact and creates one or more beliefs about this event.

Potential beliefs that might develop include:
1. "I'm not allowed to have fun. Having fun is bad. When I have fun, I get punished."
2. "I'm a bad boy. I make Mom angry."

3. "I'm helpless. There is nothing I can do to fix this situation."
4. "I'm not loved."

These and other potential beliefs become a part of your Master Plan, with instructions and strategies on how to avoid future, similarly painful events.

Your subconscious mind recorded the entire event, labeled it, and filed it under all the associated beliefs. Because there are instructions in the Master Plan about this event, this movie gets placed into the IC immediately. Your subconscious mind is now programmed to look for evidence to confirm these beliefs and to bring any matching details to your conscious awareness immediately.

Repetitive, Low-Intensity Emotional Events

Imagine again that you are a three-year-old, playing in your room and making a huge mess. Your mom comes into the room, sees the mess, and says in a soft but stern voice, "Look at this mess. You're a bad boy." Your mom might take your toy away, or make you clean up your room. You were having fun, and she interrupted it.

The emotions attached to this event are lower in intensity. You might be upset, but it wasn't a significant emotional event. Still, your subconscious mind recorded it and filed this movie away in the general category of your movie library.

If this happens repeatedly, it becomes a different story. Let's say the exact scenario happens again three

days later. Your subconscious mind makes the same recording and files it away with the first one. At this point, these videos are not important yet. However, let's say it happens again two or three more times. Your conscious mind might create these beliefs:
1. "I'm not allowed to have fun. Having fun is bad. When I have fun, I get punished."
2. "I'm a bad boy. I make Mom unhappy."
3. "I'm helpless. There is nothing I can do to fix this situation."
4. "I'm not loved."

As with the significant emotional event example, if this happens repeatedly, your conscious mind will include this data in the Master Plan, instructing your subconscious mind to look for more evidence to support these beliefs.

Remember, beliefs are created whenever you have a significant emotional event, or if something keeps happening repeatedly.

Here, Take This Belief and Make It Yours

Earlier, we said that most of your beliefs were given to you. How is that possible and why is that the case?

From birth to seven years old, your conscious mind is not fully formed or fully functional yet. If you hear something repeatedly, especially if it's from someone you love or who has authority over you, you will believe what they say is the truth.

For example, if you grew up in a poor household and heard your parents fight about money constantly or heard them say things like, "It's so hard to make money," or "Those greedy rich people," you might create a belief system of:
1. Money causes people to fight.
2. It's hard to make money.
3. Rich people are greedy.

Similarly, if you grew up with an angry, woman-hating angry father who constantly said, "You can't trust women," "All women are liars," or "All women are crazy," you are likely to grow up with similar views.

Remember, significant emotional events and low-intensity, repetitive events create beliefs.

Sleuthing for Evidence

Let's pretend that the incident with the three-year-old mentioned above happened to you, and now you have a subconscious belief of "I am a bad person." Once a recording is placed into the IC, your mind is being directed to look for evidence in your everyday life to support that belief... for the rest of your life!

You carry your belief system with you wherever you go. It's like lugging a backpack around with you for the rest of your life and looking for evidence to place into it. If a friend, uncle, or aunt says, "You're a bad boy," you'll pick this information up and put it into your backpack to validate your belief system. Same with any comments from anyone else that match your beliefs.

Soon enough, you are carrying a backpack full of evidence to support why you are such a bad person! It feels heavy, burdensome, and overwhelming to have to haul this extra weight everywhere you go. You become tired, and you have no energy or motivation to do the things you want to.

Because you have the belief "I'm a bad person" in your IC, your subconscious mind will only shift data that matches that belief into your awareness. If someone said, "You are such an amazing person," either you wouldn't hear them at all or you might hear but still not believe them. In fact, you might even try to prove that the other person is wrong.

A good example of this is to think of a time when someone gave you a simple compliment that made you feel uncomfortable. How did you respond? You might have said nothing because you didn't know how to react, especially since you didn't believe what they'd said. You might have deflected that compliment, given credit to someone else, or downplayed it completely because you were uncomfortable hearing something that didn't match your beliefs. You might even have interpreted their comment as sarcasm or false flattery.

Changing Beliefs

Although much of your belief system was developed between birth to seven years old, you can create new beliefs after seven.

Any time you experience a significant emotional event once, or a low-intensity emotional event repeatedly, you can create a new belief. You can also develop new beliefs when you, on purpose, decide that you want to change.

Some beliefs are easy to change because they are within your awareness. When you are consciously aware of a particular belief, you can decide what you want to do with it. Deeply buried beliefs are much harder to change. Even then, changing your subconscious belief system is possible. It requires working with someone knowledgeable on how to help you access the contents of your subconscious mind and deliver them to your conscious awareness in a safe and gentle way.

COOL FACT: *If you are having life experiences you don't like, you can work on becoming aware of your current faulty beliefs and creating powerful new beliefs that give you the best chance of having the life experiences you want.*

60-Second Reader

1. Much of your belief system was created from birth to seven years old.
   a. Your conscious mind, the logical part of your mind, is just beginning to form and is not fully working until around seven years old.
   b. This is why little kids believe everything they see or hear.
2. Beliefs are created whenever:
   a. You have a significant emotional event.
   b. Something happens repeatedly.
3. Once you create a belief, it goes into your IC, and your subconscious mind is programmed to look for evidence to support it.
4. Although most of your beliefs were developed between birth and seven years old, you can create new beliefs after seven.
   a. Any time you experience a significant emotional event once or a low-intensity emotional event repeatedly, you can create a new belief system.
   b. You can also develop new beliefs when you, on purpose, decide you want to change.

Notes

Notes

CHAPTER 4

The Stranger Danger Protocol

How many times have you been told that if you want to accomplish something, all you have to do is use your willpower? And how many times have you tried using your willpower, and yet, you did not achieve your goals?

You might have been frustrated or disappointed with yourself. You might have even become angry or impatient with yourself. You might ultimately believe that you're a failure.

It's very common for people to start a goal with excitement and determination, then give up on it soon after. This is because their conscious desires do not match the subconscious beliefs that they have programmed into their Master Plan.

> **COOL FACT**: *Willpower doesn't work if you subconsciously believe it's not possible to achieve your goal.*

Let's use a common scenario to illustrate this. Pretend you want to lose ten pounds. Before putting your plan into motion, you read an article that inspires you. It says if you eat under fifteen hundred calories daily and exercise three times per week for thirty minutes each time, you'll lose ten pounds in two weeks or less.

You think, "Wow! All I have to do is eat less than fifteen hundred calories per day and exercise thirty minutes a day, three times a week; I'll lose ten pounds in two weeks! That seems very doable, plus it's only two weeks! I can do this!" You set off on your weight-loss path with determination and excitement.

Soon after you start this new healthy program, something shifts that inevitably stops you from moving forward in achieving your goals. That something is your subconscious mind, and it screams, "Change is scary; change is dangerous!"

Remember when we said your subconscious mind's primary aim is to keep you safe? Well, safe doesn't mean "safe" according to your subconscious mind.

Your subconscious mind is programmed to accept that "safe" means "DO NOT CHANGE. CHANGE IS SCARY. CHANGE IS DANGEROUS! IF YOU TRY TO CHANGE, YOU WILL GET HURT OR BE DISAPPOINTED. STAY EXACTLY AS YOU ARE RIGHT NOW!"

Whenever you attempt to make a change that challenges your current belief system, your subconscious mind freaks out. It assumes that you are in danger, and it will do everything possible to get you back to safety.

Let's look at the weight-loss example again. For the sake of this example, pretend you are three hundred pounds and everyone in your family weighs at least three hundred pounds. Also imagine you have been struggling to lose weight all your life.

Perhaps you then read an article that motivates and inspires you to take action to lose weight again. You're excited! This is the thing that will finally help you lose weight! This is your answer!

When you decide to follow the new program, that is a conscious decision. You make a decision that matches what you truly want, and it's exciting to think about finally getting what you want!

As you start your new activities, you feel good about yourself. You feel hopeful because you are still within the "safety zone" according to your subconscious mind. As you continue to make changes, you move away from the safety zone and into a new territory, or the "danger zone." Your subconscious mind freaks out and thinks you're in danger. Since its job is to keep you safe, it will do all that it can to stop your new activity and return you to the "safety zone." To do that, it activates the "Stranger Danger Protocol."

> **COOL FACT:** The purpose of the Stranger Danger Protocol is to make you doubt yourself, scare you, or make you feel bad by reliving past failures, so YOU STOP what you're doing and go back to what feels "safe."

To persuade you to stop your new activities, your subconscious mind might play some of the old movies that cause you to doubt yourself. Movies that prompt you to ask, "What makes me think I can do this?"

"What would make me think this would even work?"

"I've tried so many things, and nothing's worked!"

"It's genetic and there's nothing I can do about it."

Or it might play fearful movies. "It will be so hard to exercise three times a week. It will aggravate my left knee again!" Or perhaps, "It will be so boring eating nothing but healthy food. I can't even be social; everyone I know only eats burgers and pizza!"

Your subconscious mind might then play movies of your past failures. Maybe you've lost five pounds in the past, only to gain ten pounds back. It will replay those old movies, causing you to re-experience the disappointments and make you feel like a failure.

Not only are the old painful movies playing in the background, but your subconscious mind will actively scan your environment, looking for evidence to show you why you will fail. And if that's not enough, your subconscious mind will create several scary "what-if" scenarios and play them for you.

If you are like most people, when you have doubts or fears, or you remember your past failures, you will stop doing those new activities and go back to your old ways. It seems too scary or even pointless to try anything new or unfamiliar.

Every time you start and stop like this, you strengthen your "I can't" belief. Soon, the belief becomes so heavy and so powerful that all you need to do is think about your goal and you'll go into an anxious state.

The Root of Most Problems

The Stranger Danger Protocol is not the only tool your subconscious mind has to keep you from changing. In your subconscious mind's library catalog are the four main themes we've mentioned: Instructional, Factual, Emotional, and General.

Within the Emotional Category are four main subcategories:
1. I'm Not Good Enough.
2. I'm Not Worthy.
3. I'm Not Loved.
4. I'm Not Safe.

We all have these four main subcategories in our IC. It is part of our Master Plan, created by us, to keep ourselves safe. It's also the root of most problems that we, as humans, encounter. How many movies you have in each subcategory and how often they get played depends on you, your beliefs, and your life experiences.

The details of your movies differ from those of other people because your movies are based on your specific life experiences and belief system. However, regardless of who you are, these four main subcategories are present in varying degrees, hidden in a dark corner, ready to unleash themselves at any moment.

In the next few chapters, we will discuss each of these beliefs further. But right now, let's imagine that one of your biggest beliefs, or emotional subcategories, is, "I'm not good enough." Because this is a significant belief, it is housed in your IC, and your subconscious mind is programmed to constantly look for evidence to support this. No matter where you are, no matter what you are doing, no matter who you're with, your subconscious mind is constantly looking for evidence to support the premise that you're not good enough.

Imagine in the background of your mind is a movie playing on a repetitive loop, 24/7, of all the instances that prove you're not good enough. This movie plays on and on, getting louder and louder as you attempt to do anything that might threaten or contradict this belief.

Imagine that 24/7, you are receiving messages of "You're not good enough." These constant negative thoughts and feelings keep you stuck. The fear and doubts that often accompany these messages prevent you from taking action and moving forward because it seems too scary or pointless to fight a losing battle.

Most of the time, you are unaware of the movies your subconscious mind is playing in the background for you. However, as you continue to challenge any significant belief, the applicable movies grow louder and more vivid; you might even have a conscious awareness of some of them. But most of the time, you are not fully aware of the exact cause of your underlying belief system. You might have a feeling of fear, anxiety, or discomfort that you can't fully explain.

Taming Your Subconscious Mind

What do you do when you want to change an underlying belief? How can you change your behaviors and belief system when your subconscious mind is fighting you every step of the way?

The first step is to recognize that you are the boss, and your subconscious mind is only following the instructions you have programmed into your Master Plan. Because you are the boss and you are the one responsible for programming the Master Plan, you can also change the Master Plan.

To begin, you need to acknowledge your negative emotions and decide you want to make a change. Next, create small, simple goals for yourself. In the case of the ten-pound weight loss, your small, simple goal might be to lose just one pound. Then, perhaps step it up to three pounds, then five pounds, then eight pounds, and, finally, ten pounds.

When you start on this journey, you'll initially feel good because you're doing what you consciously wanted to do, and you are within your safety zone. Soon after, you will enter the perceived danger zone, and your subconscious mind will start freaking out. It will reach for and play your old, negative movies again.

However, this time, your goal is small and simple. You push through the slight discomfort to reach your first small and simple goal. Once you reach your first goal, your subconscious mind cannot deny that you have met the goal. To keep your subconscious mind stable, you do whatever you need to do to maintain the one-pound weight loss.

Do not attempt to lose any more weight at this point. Instead, hang out at your new weight for a while, allowing your subconscious mind to realize that you are "safe" and that this is your new normal. From that new starting point, you push again until you reach the next small goal. As before, when you reach your next goal, you should just hang out there for a bit to allow your subconscious mind to establish this as a new safety zone.

How long you must wait depends on the belief you are challenging, how long that belief has been around, and the emotional charges attached to it. You will know it is time to work on the next small, simple goal when you feel comfortable, and it is effortless to maintain your current achievement.

You might be wondering, "If my conscious mind is the boss, why can't I just change the Master Plan at will? Why do I need to make these small, simple changes?"

Your conscious mind is, in fact, the boss and you can, in fact, change the parameters within the Master Plan. You can change the details within your Master Plan easily when the belief is within your awareness and of low emotional intensity.

However, when you experience something with significant negative emotions, you learn that it is too painful, and you don't want to experience that emotion again. To make sure you never encounter that pain again, you will install as many protective booby traps as possible while programming your Master Plan around that experience. This is why you must take small, simple steps to diffuse the traps without setting off the alarm.

If you take these small, simple steps in real life, it might take years to accomplish your goals, depending on what they are. We know you don't want to wait years to achieve your goals. You want to achieve your goals now, or at least in a relatively short amount of time.

The cool thing is that there are simpler, more effective ways to achieve your goals quickly. For one, you can speed up the process significantly by vividly and repeatedly imagining yourself completing your goals and completing them well. Your subconscious mind will record each time you vividly imagine yourself succeeding at your goal.

This is powerful because your subconscious mind can't tell the difference between a real event you're experiencing versus something you are vividly imagining. To your subconscious mind, it is the same. It records, sorts, and stores them both the same way.

> **COOL FACT:** *Your subconscious mind can't tell the difference between something that is happening and something you imagined. If you vividly imagine something repeatedly, your subconscious mind will believe it happened each time.*

You can use this information to your advantage. Let's say you have a goal to be comfortable and confident while doing a class presentation. Vividly imagine yourself standing in front of the classroom, feeling good about yourself, and feeling confident that you know your material well. Vividly see yourself presenting with a strong voice, making great eye contact, and feeling at ease. Vividly imagine yourself completing the presentation, answering questions with authority and confidence, and having fun in the process.

As you imagine these scenarios, bring in as much detail as you can. Use all your senses. See it. Touch it. Hear it. Taste it. Smell it. Feel the emotions attached to it. The more details that you provide, the better your recording will be and the quicker the change will occur.

Sports stars have been using this technique for centuries with amazing results! A tennis star, for example, might vividly imagine himself performing a perfect serve repeatedly—perhaps twenty times before a match. When he steps onto the court for his first serve, his mind thinks it is the twenty-first serve. His mind is calm and focused. His body is relaxed. He carries out his serve with confidence and power. This simple little technique can help you achieve any goal in your life easier and quicker.

While this technique is very useful in helping you achieve many of your goals, other goals are harder to accomplish with this method alone, especially if they are deeply rooted in your belief system. For example, if your father was abusive and left when you were nine years old, it might seem almost impossible to forgive him. You can certainly use the visualization technique mentioned above and achieve your goals, but that could take significant effort and dedication because of all the booby traps you have laid around this belief.

In instances of deep-rooted, especially traumatic beliefs, it is best to involve the guidance of a highly trained professional who specializes in addressing the subconscious mind. They can help you identify your faulty belief, its source, and the negative emotions attached to it, so you can release it successfully. Once the negative emotions are identified and released, the belief becomes neutralized; you are then free to reprogram that part of the Master Plan.

> *COOL FACT: When your conscious and subconscious minds are in conflict, your subconscious mind always wins. This is why you might struggle with things that seem easy to others. You likely have a faulty belief that's holding you back BUT you can do something to change it!*

To be successful in creating your desired changes, you must resolve your challenges at the root of the problem—that means addressing your subconscious mind. Failing to do so will cause you to revisit that problem repeatedly. The most effective therapies for changing deep-rooted belief systems address the subconscious mind directly.

In the coming chapters, we will share stories of some of Jacqui's real-life clients who resolved their problems quickly once they understood how to address their subconscious mind. We will share their main emotional subcategory and how it showed up in their lives. See if you can relate with one or more of them to begin your own self-discovery and healing.

60-Second Reader

1. Willpower doesn't work if the goal you want to achieve is not aligned with your subconscious belief system.
2. Your subconscious mind's primary aim is to keep you safe.
    a. Safe doesn't mean "safe" according to your subconscious mind.
    b. To your subconscious mind, change is scary. Change is dangerous.
    c. Whenever you attempt to change something that disrupts your current belief system, your subconscious mind freaks out. It thinks you're in danger and it will do everything it can to get you back to your "safe" place.
3. Your subconscious mind uses the Stranger Danger Protocol to get you back to your "safe" spot.
    a. The Stranger Danger Protocol will make you doubt yourself, make you fearful, or make you feel bad by reliving past failures, so YOU STOP what you're doing and go back to where it feels "safe" again.
4. Most problems can be traced back to one or more of four faulty disempowering beliefs:
    a. "I'm not good enough."
    b. "I'm not worthy."

       c. "I'm not loved."
       d. "I'm not safe."
5. To tame your subconscious mind, start by being the boss of your mind. Give your subconscious mind clear and direct commands.
       a. Create small, simple goals that lead to the ultimate big goal to prevent the Stranger Danger Protocol from being activated.
6. Your subconscious mind cannot tell the difference between what's real and what's imagined. To your subconscious mind, they are the same.
       a. Whatever you want to achieve, vividly imagine yourself already achieving that goal. Be sure to attach strong, positive emotions as you imagine your achievements to help your subconscious mind quickly accept it as "safe."
       b. This simple technique can help you achieve any goal in your life easier and quicker.
7. When your conscious and subconscious minds are in conflict, your subconscious mind always wins.

Notes

Notes

Case Studies

CHAPTER 5

I'm Not Good Enough

"I'm not good enough" is the emotional subcategory that's easiest to identify in your movie library. At the root of many problems is an underlying belief that you're not good enough.

Before you dismiss this notion as a possibility, realize that this belief often hides under the surface of your conscious thinking and can still be a significant source of trouble for you.

This belief might show up as:
- "I'm not [insert your word here] enough (i.e., smart, tall, good-looking, funny, talented, strong etc.)."
- "I can't seem to do anything right."
- "Others are always doing better than I am."
- "I have nothing important to contribute."
- "There is something wrong with me."
- "I'm not good at anything."

Case Study: Stressed-Out Steve
Client: Steve, Age 19

Presenting Problem

Steve has come in for help because his anxiety and negative attitude have been getting worse. He has no energy or interest in things he used to find fun. Even the most trivial daily tasks have become difficult for him. Most recently, he has become very fearful of driving and makes excuses to avoid going onto the freeway.

Family History

Steve lives at home with his parents and his younger brother, Brian. Steve recalls never feeling very loved or valued in his family. He doesn't get along with Brian and, in fact, feels significant anger and resentment towards him.

Brian has always been the favorite child, regardless of how much mischief or trouble he causes. In fact, Brian struggles in school and has been skipping classes and even experimenting with drugs and alcohol over the past year. Even so, Brian is the one their parents have showered love and affection upon.

Social History

Steve recently graduated with honors from high school and is attending a local university on a full scholarship.

Steve has always excelled academically, not because he is naturally gifted, but because this is the one area in which his parents acknowledge him and show approval for his efforts. It is also an area that Steve feels he has control over. In addition, since Brian struggles with a mild learning disability, it is easier for Steve to shine and be known as the "smart one" of the brothers.

Steve has a few friends that he used to hang out with. Socially, he has never fit in because his family is poor, and he was bussed to a rich neighborhood for school. This has made it difficult for Steve to make and keep friends, both because of the economic differences and the physical distance of his classmates' homes.

Words Others Often Use to Describe Steve

Smart, gifted, serious, dependable, hard worker

Words Steve Uses to Describe Himself

Anxious, stressed out, inferior, insignificant, fearful

Session One Notes

Steve is a good-natured young man who is very likable. He is polite and well spoken, although he often apologizes for what he is saying or thinking.

Steve is most bothered by the fact that he has become quite anxious while driving. Driving was something Steve used to love doing, relying on that activity as an escape from his family and his stressful life events. Steve recalls loving the feeling of the wind against his face and arm, as his stereo blasts his favorite music.

All this changed when he got into a car accident six months ago. He doesn't remember what happened exactly. He must have looked down to change the music or something, and when he looked up, he was surprised to see the car in front of him had come to a complete stop. Steve didn't have enough time to react and slammed into the back of the other vehicle.

The sounds of the crunching metal and the screeching tires terrified him. Steve didn't know what to do. He was completely frozen.

The other driver got out of his car and aggressively walked toward Steve, yelling profanities and making threatening gestures. The whole incident felt surreal to Steve. He doesn't remember much of what happened next, nor how he was able to drive himself home.

Steve was still in shock when he arrived home. Life had been rough as of late with the increasing anxiety and fear, but the car accident was definitely the most frightening experience he had had. Steve just wanted to sleep this nightmare away.

The moment he drifted off to sleep, however, he was awakened by a screaming voice. "How could you be so irresponsible?" his father yelled. "You borrowed my car, and this is what you do? Don't you ever think about how your actions will affect anyone else?"

Steve was speechless. Yes, he had gotten into a car accident, and the car was damaged, but he couldn't believe his dad hadn't stopped to make sure he was okay before aggressively attacking him.

"What about me?" he wanted to yell back at his dad. "Don't I mean anything to you?"

For the rest of the session, we talk about how this incident has affected Steve and work on resolving some of his anger toward his father.

Sessions Two and Three Notes

Steve comes back determined to learn to be comfortable driving again. He reports that each time he thinks about driving, he replays the accident and its aftermath in his head. He admits to being unable to shut off the sound of the crunching metal and the screeching tires, not to mention the cruelty of his father's reaction.

Fortunately, because the events were so specific and vivid, we are able to use a simple technique to scramble those movies in his mind's library so that he has a difficult time accessing and replaying them. This process can be likened to taking a DVD movie and scratching the back of it, causing it to skip and, eventually, to not play at all.

After scrambling his movies, Steve tries his best to replay them but can't. He beams at this success.

We then spend some time using vivid imagery to help Steve feel comfortable driving again and practice how to stop his stress and anxiety.

Session Four Notes

Steve is now feeling more comfortable behind the wheel and has even started driving on the freeway. Although he still chooses to drive for less than ten minutes on the freeway, he feels in control of this situation. He wants to do the rest of the work on his own so we can make progress on his other anxieties and lack of motivation.

Root Cause

A consistent theme for Steve growing up was struggling hard to gain his parents' attention and affection. His mother was always busy working and taking care of the house, so she rarely had time to spend just with him. His father was unpredictable. Most of the time, he would ignore Steve; other times, he would get angry at Steve for no apparent reason. The only time he seemed to approve of Steve was when he brought home good grades from school. This has caused Steve to always strive to do his best academically in order to gain his dad's approval.

Steve recalls that before Brian was born, his mother would spend time reading to him at bedtime. These were the best, most valued moments to Steve as it was the only time his mother gave him her undivided attention. Steve treasured those moments and did his very best to earn even more time with her.

When Steve was six years old, his mother told him she was pregnant, and he would soon have a little brother. Steve had been jealous of his friends who had siblings to play with, so when he heard this news, he was very excited and happy.

That happiness was short-lived, however. Right after announcing the good news, his mother shared something that devastated Steve. She told him that because there would be a new addition to the family, she would quit her job to take care of the baby.

Steve immediately sensed an overwhelming mix of sadness, anger, and jealousy. He could not believe that he had been trying so hard to get his mother's attention and his effort hadn't paid off. Yet, this little brother of his had already won her love and affection and he wasn't even born yet!

At that moment, Steve felt:
1. Unloved: "My mom doesn't love me. She doesn't give me any attention."
2. Jealous: "It's so unfair. He (the baby) doesn't have to do anything to be loved."
3. Anger at himself: "Something is wrong with me. I must be a bad kid. I'm unlovable."
4. Fear: "Mom will only love the baby. She will forget about me."

For the rest of the night, Steve tried his best to understand why he wasn't enough. If Steve had ever thought he wasn't good enough before, this incident had certainly validated it for him.

Brian, meanwhile, was full of trouble and mischief right from birth. He cried constantly and demanded his mother's full attention. His mother spent most of her day taking care of Brian, leaving her with less time and energy for Steve. The nightly reading ritual that Steve treasured so much became less frequent.

When Steve caught on that crying got his mother's attention, he became very clingy and threw a minor tantrum whenever he wanted some of his mother's focus. At first, it seemed as if this ploy had worked because his mother would stop fussing over Brian long enough to check on him.

That tactic quickly backfired, though, as his mother became impatient and irritated with Steve's behavior. She would often say, "You need to stop acting like a baby. I don't have time for this nonsense. I have to take care of Brian." This was further proof to Steve that he wasn't enough, and that Brian meant everything to her.

As Brian got older, the trouble escalated. Brian would disrupt his classes, get into fights, and even outwardly disobey the teachers. Even with this bad behavior, Brian continued to get all their parents' attention and affection.

Steve recalls being so angry and jealous every time the three of them would huddle together and talk for hours about what Brian could do to make everyone happier. When Brian showed any hint of "normal" behavior, their parents would act as if it were the best thing ever. They would even have a family celebration, during which Brian was praised continuously for making their parents so proud and happy.

Steve hated himself for not being enough to earn his parents' love and also hated Brian for receiving all their attention and affection.

Sessions Five to Eight Notes

We then spend the next four sessions working on releasing Steve's belief that he isn't enough and helping him to see his life situations differently.

At first, Steve is unwilling to let go of his anger and resentment toward Brian, but with encouragement,

Steve learns to perceive those situations in a more positive light.

When he was six, Steve felt his mother's declaration of "staying home to take care of the baby" was a direct insult and injustice to him. Looking back, he can fully understand why she chose to stay home. After doing the math, he acknowledges his mother's income did not justify her continued work because most of her wages would have gone straight to the costs of daycare. Steve can also see that her decision to stay home was not only for Brian, but for the whole family—himself included.

As for Brian, Steve has learned to see him differently as well and become more compassionate toward him. He and his brother were both raised by an angry, verbally abusive dad and a mother who was too weak to stand up to him. To cope, Brian took it out on other people. Brian didn't know any better; he was simply modeling his father's behaviors.

Steve now understands that the reason Brian received so much attention wasn't because his parents favored him, but because Brian needed more help.

Rather than viewing Brian as a spoiled brat who tricked their parents into thinking he's perfect, Steve sees that Brian is, in fact, very wounded and has needed constant positive reinforcement just to stay afloat.

Steve also realizes that his parents trusted him and his ability to take care of himself. Their actions weren't due to a lack of love, but simply relief that at least one of their sons was doing well. This revelation has given Steve tremendous comfort and allowed him to start seeing the positive qualities in himself.

Two-Month Follow-Up

Steve is driving normally again. Being able to conquer that fear has given Steve a new sense of confidence in himself. He loves the freedom driving provides him, allowing him to go where and when he wants to. This has also enabled Steve to establish lasting friendships.

Steve reports that his relationship is much better with his mother. Since his sessions ended, Steve and his mother have committed to spending quality time together at least twice a week. This has given mother and son a chance to get to know each other better and to bond more deeply.

As for Brian, Steve was surprised to learn that his brother also resented him significantly. Brian revealed that he was always jealous of "perfect" Steve, who could do no wrong. This realization has helped the brothers mend their relationship as they start to discover more about each other.

Steve's relationship with his father, however, has not changed. His father continues to ignore Steve (and the rest of the family, as Steve now realizes). The main difference today is that Steve doesn't take it personally. Instead, he chooses to focus on strengthening his relationships with his mother, brother, and friends.

Lesson Learned

Being raised in an environment with so much emotional tension and so little personal attention had a negative impact on Steve's beliefs about himself. For as long as Steve could remember, he felt as if he wasn't enough and that there was something wrong with him. The only thing Steve thought he had going for himself was his academic record. Unfortunately, Steve was not a naturally gifted student, and the pressure he put on himself to excel caused significant stress.

Since Steve had a belief that he wasn't good enough, he was always seeking approval and validation from others. The moment something went wrong, Steve would verbally beat himself up. This tore down his confidence even more and caused his emotional state to further deteriorate, thus reinforcing his negative beliefs.

Once he identified and neutralized the pain attached to the faulty beliefs of a little boy, he could see the situation for what it was and recognize the errors within his belief system.

The problem wasn't that he wasn't enough; the problem was that his parents thought he WAS enough (old enough, responsible enough, smart enough, etc.) to take care of himself, so they devoted more attention to helping his younger brother learn to be more like him. Unfortunately, they could not convey that in a way that Steve could understand at that age.

COOL FACT: There are always more sides to the story than just your side, and things are most often not what they seem at first.

When things are not going well for you, rather than focusing on what's wrong and making the problem bigger, ask yourself, "How can I see this situation differently?" Have fun with this question. Be a detective and look for clues that point to the possibilities of different conclusions, especially happier ones.

When you have a strong negative reaction to something, you can bet that there is an underlying belief at play. Be willing to pause, examine the situation, and identify the potential negative beliefs (or "triggers" for your feelings). Be willing to let go of your original thoughts or beliefs and become open to seeing evidence of the new (and improved) conclusions you've just created. You might find yourself pleasantly surprised.

Self-Reflection

What is your biggest takeaway from this chapter?

How can you use what you've just learned to take charge of your mind and be a happier, more confident you?

CHAPTER 6

I'm Not Worthy

Many times, the "I'm not good enough" and "I'm not worthy" beliefs go hand in hand. It often looks like this: "I don't deserve_____ because I'm not _____." It can also appear as "I don't deserve _____ because I am (something negative)."

This belief might show up as:
- "I don't deserve to be successful because I'm not a hard enough worker."
- "I don't deserve this award because I'm not smart."
- "I don't deserve to have friends because I'm a burden to others."

"I'm not worthy" can also result from having guilty feelings because of something you have done in the past:
- "I don't deserve to get into the top college because I cheated on the entrance exam."

- "I don't deserve to be happy because I've hurt so many people in the past."

Case Study: Bored Brandon
Client: Brandon, Age 16

Presenting Problem

Brandon was recently diagnosed with depression and anxiety. His doctor started him on Prozac, which he stopped taking after a few days because it made him feel "numb." He also thought the Prozac made it more difficult for him to think and concentrate.

Brandon's parents are concerned because Brandon has been suffering from "excessive worrying and catastrophic thinking." It doesn't matter where he is, or what is happening around him, Brandon is an expert at finding every little problem or potential for trouble. His mind becomes consumed with how to fix these imagined problems and ways to avoid potential negative outcomes. It has gotten so bad that Brandon rarely leaves his room, preferring to spend most of his time alone, writing new programs on his computer.

Brandon reports not knowing why his parents and doctor think he's depressed. He insists he's just bored, and everything is fine. The only reason he agreed to come in was that his parents threatened to take his computer away if he didn't get help.

Family History

Brandon is the youngest child of a large family. He reports having had a good childhood. His parents are older, and most of Brandon's siblings have moved out of the house. While Brandon gets along with his family, he doesn't feel close to anyone, including his parents.

When Brandon was seven, his father took a new job, which prompted a move to another state. A few months later, his family moved back, only to relocate once more for another job the following fall.

Social History

Brandon reports making friends easily but hasn't had any close friends for several years. Brandon doesn't have a girlfriend. He says he's very picky, and not really interested in the girls he knows because they are "not worth the trouble." He spends most of his free time on the computer at home where he has taught himself to write programs. Brandon often stays up late working on his computer because he has trouble sleeping.

Words Others Often Use to Describe Brandon

Smart, funny, calm, thoughtful, kind

Words Brandon Uses to Describe Himself

Loner, bored, frustrated, in my head, intellect, different than others, insomniac

Session One Notes

Brandon is engaging and well spoken. He talks easily about facts, computers, and observations he has about school, his family, and society. Brandon is unsure why his doctor diagnosed him with depression. He thinks it's normal that he prefers to work on developing new programs instead of hanging out with people. When he's out in social settings, Brandon is often distracted, thinking about potential problems and wishing he were home. Brandon reports that he gets bored so easily, to the point that he's often "in his head." Unfortunately, that causes him to miss out on conversations and feel awkward whenever someone asks him something specific. Occasionally, he does catch himself in a good mood, but he's quick to remind himself not to feel so happy because it won't last. He likes to be "realistic" about that.

Session Three Notes

Brandon is very hesitant to share personal details during his sessions. Instead, he talks endlessly about computers and computer programming.

It takes a lot of effort to get Brandon to participate in any talks about his feelings. Brandon does not like discussing them, as he sees feelings as either unnecessary or a sign of weakness. He says that feelings don't matter, because "things are how they are" and he needs to just deal with it. Occasionally, Brandon will slip and mention that he feels sad or lonely. However, he quickly dismisses those feelings with, "I'm just bored. There's nothing to challenge me."

Session Five Notes

Brandon has come in today after a big fight with his mom. For the first thirty minutes, Brandon talks nonstop about how angry he is that his mom took his computer away, even though he's been coming in for his weekly sessions, as agreed. When pressed for more details, Brandon shares that his parents have tried to force him to attend a fundraiser for their local Boys and Girls Club. Even though Brandon knows the money raised is going to help start a computer club for the kids, he is also painfully aware of how awkward the event will be. Brandon's father is a big man with an even bigger personality. He talks and laughs loudly and doesn't seem to understand personal space. His mother, conversely, is a stern woman who rarely smiles. Being around his parents always embarrasses Brandon because he is certain that everyone is judging him and his family.

Brandon imagines that his father will begin making "dad jokes" and telling embarrassing stories about him. Brandon is also concerned that his mother will come off as snobby or cold to the other attendees. Her attitude always embarrasses Brandon. Brandon is uncomfortable because he's so afraid of what people might say about him and his parents. Besides, Brandon reasons, he doesn't have the right clothes for the event and his shoes are in bad shape. Brandon doesn't want anyone to look down on him for his lack of style.

For the rest of the session, we spend time reviewing how the mind works and how his fear of being judged has triggered his mind to work overtime to create that experience for him. The new insights pique his curiosity to learn more about how past experiences can affect him now, and to understand how his mind operates.

Root Cause

Feeling more open, Brandon is willing to explore the causes behind his negativity and catastrophic thinking.

When asked what he thinks was his most difficult experience growing up, Brandon shares a story of his family's first move to a big city when he was in the second grade. Brandon's new classmates seemed more mature than his old friends. They also had nicer clothes and lived in fancier houses. Brandon felt so uncomfortable around them. He knew he didn't fit in.

For the first couple days of school, Brandon stuck to himself. Even though he felt lonely, Brandon had convinced himself that it was better to be alone. On the third day of school, however, a pretty girl named Sally said she wanted to be his friend.

For the next couple of days, Brandon followed Sally around and did whatever Sally told him to do. Brandon didn't care that Sally was bossing him around. He was merely relieved to have someone to hang out with.

During recess one day, Sally told Brandon she wanted him to call her "Princess." Brandon thought it was strange but decided to do as Sally asked.

Reluctantly, he whispered "Princess". This was unacceptable to Sally, who then demanded that Brandon bow to her and loudly call her "Princess."

Not wanting to make a scene, Brandon quickly bowed and repeated "Princess" a little louder this time. Unfortunately for Brandon, a few boys in his class happened to walk by at that exact moment and laughed at Brandon. They started making fun of Brandon and asking him if he thought a hillbilly like himself deserved a princess.

Sally laughed loudly and said, "No way! He doesn't deserve a princess. He doesn't deserve anything. He's just a stupid boy I was bossing around for fun." And with that, his only friend took off without so much as a glance back his way.

This started a daily ritual of the boys bullying Brandon and making him feel weak. The bullies would find new ways to embarrass Brandon, especially around Sally. Each time, Sally would join in the harassment.

Brandon felt confused, hurt, and angry. He wanted to say something, but each time he opened his mouth to defend himself, no words would come out. His classmates noticed Brandon's failed attempts to defend himself and made fun of him even more. Brandon felt ashamed for not being able to stick up for himself.

With each passing day, Brandon became more fearful. He was scared to go to school but didn't know how to tell his parents. Luckily, his parents told him they were moving back to his old hometown.

Brandon was so excited to move back and reconnect with his former friends. He had visions of the "good old days," where life was simple, and he was well liked.

To Brandon's surprise, however, when he moved back, it seemed that his old friends had all changed. They had inside jokes that Brandon was not a part of. They didn't laugh at any of Brandon's jokes either. Even though they tried to include him in their conversations, Brandon felt like he no longer belonged. When Brandon hung out with his friends, he felt like a "huge burden and a loser."

This made Brandon feel alone and lonely, even when he was with his friends. Over time, Brandon stopped hanging out with his friends at school and would decline invitations to after-school get-togethers. Instead, he preferred to be alone with a book, or messing around on his computer.

Brandon was relieved when his parents told him they were moving again. And even though Brandon didn't know how, he was determined to re-invent himself and become a more likable person at his next school.

Before moving, Brandon created a whole new persona. He was starting third grade at a new school, and he wanted to make sure it was perfect. Brandon decided the best way for him to fit in was to pay attention to his clothes, hairstyle, and posture. He made sure to present himself at his best and even made up stories to make himself look even better. He also showcased his accomplishments in computer programming by sharing games he had created. Before long, many of Brandon's classmates were hanging out at the school library with him during lunch to learn how to create simple games.

Brandon was so excited that his plan had worked. Everyone seemed to like him at the new school. Even the most popular girl, Amanda, was talking to him.

Soon, Amanda and Brandon started "going together," as his friends called it. Brandon was happier than he had been in a long time. Everything he had ever wanted had finally come true.

But then, the unthinkable happened one day. For reasons unknown to Brandon, Amanda decided to break up with him. Instead of telling him privately, Amanda wrote a note and asked her friend, Cheryl who was sitting a few seats in front of Brandon, to give it to him. Cheryl opened the note, read it, and laughed. She passed it to the next student, who also read it, laughed, and passed it to the next student, and on down the line.

Brandon had no idea that the note was about him. He was eager to read the message because he wanted to be included in whatever was so funny. When it finally got to him, Brandon was mortified. The note said, "Brandon, I don't want to be your girlfriend anymore."

Brandon was too embarrassed to even look up, as he knew at least four people had read that note before it reached him. Brandon wasn't sure what was worse—that his girl had dumped him or that everyone had known about it before he did!

The whole room was spinning. Brandon could barely see straight. It was hard for him to breathe. At that moment, Brandon felt:
1. Angry with himself: "I'm so dumb. How could I not realize what was happening?"
2. Humiliated: "Everyone knew what was happening, and I didn't even have a clue."
3. Sad: "I thought Amanda liked me. I thought my friends liked me."

4. Confused: "Why does this keep happening to me? What did I do to deserve this?"
5. Scared: "Am I going to be bullied again?"
6. Unworthy: "I'm worthless. No one likes me."

As Brandon sat there fighting back the tears, Sally's words and laughter echoed loudly in his head: "He doesn't deserve anything. He's just a stupid boy!"

When the class ended, Brandon stayed behind. He didn't want to face anyone because he was dealing with so much shame, sadness, and humiliation.

That night, Brandon could not fall asleep. He replayed every event he could remember between him and Amanda, looking for the missing puzzle piece. Why did she break up with him? Why did she allow everyone to know before him? What about him was so terrible? How did he not see this coming? How could he be so stupid? His mind scrambled for all potential clues about what he could have done differently to prevent this terrible event. He felt sick to his stomach as he continued to replay every single detail of this painful episode, ultimately thinking Sally was right: "I don't deserve anything good. I'm just a stupid boy."

Brandon felt completely foolish for believing it would somehow be different at this school... that he would finally fit in and be happy.

During our sessions, these memories take Brandon by surprise as he hasn't thought about them for many years. What surprises him most is how much shame, sadness, and anger he is feeling and reliving right now.

Using some specific visualization techniques, Brandon realizes his feelings of unworthiness have caused him to miss out on so many fun events and great people over the years. His subconscious mind was convinced there was danger in social interactions and friendships, so he closed himself off from others to prevent further rejections. Brandon has finally made the connection between these painful past events and his current attitude towards friendship, himself, and life.

Brandon is also surprised by how disappointed he is at himself for not standing up for himself in the past.

Sessions Six to Nine Notes

Throughout the next few sessions, Brandon slowly realizes how he's been using his computer and programming as a shield to protect himself from potential hurts. Before now, Brandon had no idea how much his experiences with the bullies had affected him.

After significant reassurance, Brandon is willing to accept that he was just a young boy then, doing the best he could at the time to get through his challenging situations. For the next few sessions, we work on forgiving those who caused him pain, as well as forgiving himself for any action or inactions that resulted in his unhappy outcome.

Two-Month Follow-Up

Brandon comes in with a big smile on his face. Instead of hiding away in his room and programming, he has signed up to volunteer to teach coding at the local Boys and Girls Club. Brandon loves teaching others and uses this opportunity to help other "lost little Brandons" to feel accepted and supported.

Brandon reports he has a new positive outlook on life and feels so relieved that he no longer has to be on hyper-alert for every little potential problem. When he catches himself with catastrophic thinking, Brandon quickly reminds himself to let it go and to focus his attention on something else.

Lesson Learned

Although Brandon hadn't thought about the incident with Sally and the subsequent bullying for many years, those events were significant for him emotionally and had created a strong belief of "I'm not worthy" and "I'm not smart enough (I'm stupid)." The incident with Amanda was further proof, which only strengthened those faulty beliefs.

Once he created the belief that he was unworthy and not enough, he unknowingly programmed his mind to look for evidence to support those beliefs. His mind did exactly what he had instructed it to do and made him hyper-aware of every incident that matched his belief system. To protect himself, Brandon avoided situations where he could be rejected, and he put himself on hyper-alert for any potential trouble.

When you hold on to emotions such as fear, guilt, and self-blame, you often suffer needlessly. Forgiveness is the most effective way to release the pain and give yourself a clean slate. When you forgive yourself for your response (or lack of response), you release those heavy feelings that stop you from enjoying yourself. Forgiving others is also an important step to setting yourself free. Forgiving yourself or others doesn't mean that you condone what happened, nor that you think it's okay. To forgive means you understand that the situation happened, but it does not define who you are, and it doesn't have to dictate what you can or cannot do. You release the power that those past situations have over you so you can move forward with your life and focus on what you decide is important.

> ***COOL FACT:*** *If having negative feelings about yourself is stopping you from doing what brings you happiness, now is the right time to let them go. Give yourself permission to release these harmful emotions and forgive yourself. You do not need to hang on to the pain to avoid the same mistake, or to "learn your lesson." Once you have forgiven yourself, you free yourself to follow the path you truly want to take.*

Self-Reflection

What is your biggest takeaway from this chapter?

How can you use what you've just learned to take charge of your mind and be a happier, more confident you?

CHAPTER 7

I'm Not Loved

As humans, we all have a strong need to feel loved and be connected to others. Love is such an important emotion that it drives many of our thoughts and actions. When we feel loved and connected, life seems easier somehow. Without love, we often feel alone, lonely, and incomplete.

"I'm not loved" often shows up as:
- "No one likes me."
- "I'm all alone in this world."
- "Everybody abandoned me."
- "I'm unlovable."
- "Who would love me?"
- "Everyone hates me."
- "I hate myself."

Case Study: Worrisome Wyatt
Client: Wyatt, Age 15

Presenting Problem

Wyatt's parents, Ann and Michael, brought him in for help because over the past year Wyatt has become increasingly withdrawn, anxious, and angry. They report that he has become so anxious and uncomfortable with social situations that he now finds it difficult to eat in public settings. His mother reports that he is so fearful of being judged or criticized that he refrains from expressing himself but will then "explode" uncontrollably when things become too much.

Ann has been pleading with Wyatt to get help, but he has refused. He is convinced that nobody understands him, and that counseling would be a waste of time. Wyatt finally gave in to his mother's requests after realizing that he was rapidly losing weight and that his angry outbursts were becoming more frequent and more explosive. Wyatt was afraid he was losing his mind and would end up in a mental institution, just as one of his uncles had.

Family History

Ann and Michael adopted Wyatt when he was six months old, though he didn't learn of the adoption until he turned eight years old. Over the years, Ann and Michael have done their best to treat Wyatt with the same love and care they've given their older, biological son, William. In fact, they've often overcompensated with Wyatt, to the dismay of William.

Even though Ann and Michael are loving and supportive parents, and William has been as good a brother as one could expect, Wyatt hasn't felt completely loved or accepted by any of them since finding out that he was adopted. Instead, he feels more like an outsider who doesn't fit in with a house full of "normal, happy people," as he calls them.

Social History

Wyatt has a large group of friends whom he has known for many years. Lately, he has been distancing himself from them because he feels that he is a burden to his friends and believes they only hang out with him out of pity and habit.

When they are together, Wyatt is withdrawn and irritable. He wants to join in on the conversations and the fun, but he is too afraid that his thoughts might be made fun of or, even worse, rejected. Instead, he just sits silently with them, all the while replaying in his mind the many things he feels he has done wrong—along with all the "stupid" comments he has made.

Wyatt is convinced that everything he does is annoying to his friends, including how he chews his food. In fact, a few friends teased him about doing just that a few months ago. Since then, he can no longer eat when his friends are around, or even in a public place where others might see him chewing. This has resulted in Wyatt becoming less social, as well as skipping meals, which has led to his rapid weight loss.

Words Others Often Use to Describe Wyatt

Smart, talented, quiet, shy, nice

Words Wyatt Uses to Describe Himself

Loner, loser, stupid, burdensome, misfit

Session One Notes

Wyatt is a quiet young man who makes very little eye contact when we first meet. He sits on the couch, wringing his hands and shifting in his seat nonstop.

Wyatt loves his adoptive parents, whom he calls "parents," not "adoptive parents." He believes that they are trying very hard to love him. He also believes that he should be grateful for his situation, but at the same time, he feels the burden of living up to being a perfect son—someone who is deserving of being "chosen." This, he thinks, he cannot do. After all, Wyatt sees himself as incapable of having anything positive to contribute to his family or society. He believes that his birth parents gave him up because he was unlovable and that he doesn't have much genuine value.

Wyatt spends most of the session ranting on and on about his supposed faults, expressing anger at himself for being so burdensome to others. He doesn't understand why he cannot relate to other people and why other people seem unable to relate to him.

Initially, Wyatt does not want to talk about being adopted, but toward the end of the session, he quietly says, "I can't relate to other people because I wasn't meant to be here. My birth parents didn't want me. I must have been such a burden to them." With that statement, Wyatt refuses to elaborate on his birth parents or the adoption.

We then spend the rest of the session discussing calming techniques and creating an outline of what Wyatt wants to accomplish during our time together. At the top of Wyatt's list is, "how to stop being a burden."

Session Two Notes

Wyatt has come in with the same low energy and shyness that he displayed the week prior; his eye contact is just as absent. When asked what's wrong, Wyatt states that he thinks agreeing to come here was a mistake and that he's certain there is no help for him.

When pressed to provide more details, Wyatt states that it was his fate to be this way, that he was born a burden, and there's nothing that will change that situation. With that, Wyatt stands up and walks toward the door to leave.

With one hand on the doorknob and his back facing the room, Wyatt asks quietly, "Be honest. Can you help someone like me? Do I have any hope?"

After some reassurance that he can be helped and that he is not alone in how he feels, Wyatt sits back down and cries. Through his tears, he expresses that he is so tired of feeling like a burden. All he wants to do is to be a good person, someone his parents will be proud of. Wyatt desperately wants to be someone that people can count on.

Feeling hopeful, Wyatt talks and cries for a while. When he is done, Wyatt looks up and says, "You told me you could help me. It's hard to trust people, but I will try to trust you because I just want to be a good person."

And with that, Wyatt starts sharing his deeper fears. His biggest fear is that he was born unlovable and that there is nothing good in him. Wyatt believes that no matter how hard he tries, all he does is make people mad or let them down. He is terrified of disappointing his parents, and that they too will leave him, just like his birth parents did.

Root Cause

On his eighth birthday, Wyatt received a water gun that he'd desperately wanted. It was one of those water guns that can spray a stream of water across a long distance. Wyatt and his brother, William, were in the backyard, having a water fight. Wyatt had his new super water gun and William had a regular, not-as-powerful water gun. Wyatt had so much fun playing with his new gun that when William stopped playing, Wyatt became irritated. How could William stop the fun?

As William walked away and headed toward the house, Wyatt yelled angrily, "You're a wimp. You're quitting because I have a better gun." As he yelled that, he ran up toward William and shot him with his water gun, just in time for William to turn around and take a large burst of water right in the face.

Wyatt knew he was in trouble the moment he saw William's eyes. He had never seen William that angry before. For some unknown reason, rather than backing down, Wyatt felt a stronger urge to continue his shooting and name-calling.

William angrily grabbed the water gun and yelled, "Just shut up. I hate you." He then pushed Wyatt down and threw the water gun at his head.

This angered Wyatt even more. He got up, pushed William hard, and threatened, "Just wait. I'm going to tell Mom and Dad. You're going to be in big trouble."

The next thing that happened was the worst moment in Wyatt's life up to that point. William grabbed him, picked him up, and yelled, "Go ahead, you little shit! Do you think they are really going to be on your side? You're so stupid! You don't even know... they're not even your real parents. You're adopted! Your own parents don't even want you. That's how stupid you really are!"

Horrified, Wyatt shook free. He didn't believe the words that had just come out of his brother's mouth. How could he be so cruel? Why would his brother make up such a horrible story? He didn't want to believe what he'd just heard. It just couldn't be true.

The moment he looked at William's fearful expression and heard William beg him not to tell their parents what he'd just said, Wyatt knew that William had, in fact, told him the truth.

Wyatt didn't know what to do. All he knew at that moment was that he needed to get out of there. He began to run away from the house as fast as he could—although he had no clue where he was going. He just knew he had to get out of there.

Wyatt ended up at a public park several blocks away from the house. He hid behind some bushes so that no one could see him. He did not want to be found. He needed to sort things out for himself.

As he sat there thinking about the past, he replayed the painful memories of fights, anger, and disappointments. Wyatt recalled all the family gatherings where everyone seemed to have fun, except him. Wyatt never felt that he knew what to say. Each time he tried to join in the conversation, his family would look at him as if he were an alien life form and then return to their conversations with one another. He felt so excluded and alone.

In that instant, everything made sense! Wyatt finally understood why he was the family outcast. And the moment he determined that he was the family outcast, he became furious with himself and even angrier at them. "How can I be the family outcast? I'm not even a part of their family. They are a bunch of liars!"

The anger was quickly replaced with fear. Wyatt's mind raced with new worries. "If I'm not a part of their family, where do I belong? Do I have a family? Who am I? What about what William said, that my real family doesn't want me?"

At that moment, Wyatt felt:
1. Unlovable: "Nobody wants me; even my own parents didn't want me."
2. Angry: "I've been lied to all my life. I was thrown away."
3. Helpless: "I don't even know who my parents are. What am I going to do?"
4. Alone: "I have no place to go. I don't have a home. I don't have a family."

5. Unworthy: "I'm a burden. I've been a burden. Who would want me around?"
6. Foolish: "How could I not have realized the truth? I don't even look like them."

Although he didn't want to be found, Wyatt was relieved when his adoptive parents discovered him in the park and pleaded with him to come home. In that moment, they confirmed Wyatt's worst fear—that he was, in fact, adopted. Although they did their best to reassure Wyatt that he was very much loved and wanted, Wyatt could not hear it. He was certain that they were lying to him as they had been for his entire life.

This was the beginning of Wyatt's belief that he was unlovable and a burden to everyone. Although his family continued to treat him well, Wyatt found fault in everything they did and in everything he did.

As Wyatt shares his story in our session, he is very quiet, almost stoic. One would have to strain hard just to hear him.

Although Wyatt is hesitant to stay for the session, he is so ready to let go of his pain, and he does so impressively. He fully and eagerly participates in the various techniques used to help him see his past situations differently. It is so wonderful to witness Wyatt release so much pain in a single session.

Sessions Three to Eight Notes

For the next six sessions, we work on letting go of the negative emotions attached to his significant painful events. Wyatt especially loves the concept that everything that happened is simply a movie in his mind. He excels at seeing the same painful situations in a very fun and enlightened way. He loves knowing that he is the writer and director of his own movies. The new endings he creates are so imaginative and fun that we spend a large part of our time together laughing.

With each session, Wyatt becomes more and more alive. He fully embraces the concept that his old, repetitive thoughts and fears are merely bad movies playing on "repeat." The ability to "turn off" these movies helps Wyatt to feel strong and confident.

Four-Month Follow-Up

When Wyatt appears in the waiting room, he is almost unrecognizable. Since his last visit, he has gained about twenty pounds and grown several inches taller. He now looks healthy, strong, and happy.

Wyatt reports—and his parents have confirmed—that life has been the best for Wyatt these past few months. He has finally accepted that his parents do, in fact, love him as their son, not as their adopted son.

Wyatt also accepts that William has always been sincere in his actions and expression of care toward him. He finally understands that it was he who could not receive the love and affection. Wyatt no longer sees himself as an outsider or a burden to the family, but rather, he sees himself as an equally important and valued family member.

Wyatt is also doing so much better at school and with his friends. Instead of shying away from conversations and withdrawing, Wyatt has decided to just "throw it out there and see what happens." And so far, Wyatt reports, with a big grin on his face, most of his stuff sticks and it's fun to be the director of his life movies.

Lesson Learned

This is another strong lesson in how you create your own reality. The moment Wyatt learned that he was adopted, he saw himself as unloved and unlovable. Once Wyatt believed he was unloved, his subconscious mind raced to look for evidence to support his beliefs.

He looked for faults in everything and everyone. When he disobeyed and got into trouble, rather than accepting responsibility for his actions, he blamed it on the fact that he was adopted, and people were just picking on him.

His difficulty connecting with his peers stemmed from the same belief that he was unlovable. How could anyone truly want to be his friend? He had nothing to contribute; he was only a burden. Because of those beliefs, he started withdrawing into his head and creating stories to justify his actions.

The more he withdrew, the more uncomfortable he became with himself and with his friends. He became increasingly afraid of being judged as a "weirdo." This cycle perpetuated and continued to the point where he couldn't eat and lost a significant amount of weight.

When Wyatt learned that he was the writer and director of his movies, he took charge and rewrote his stories powerfully. He took full advantage of this knowledge and his new skills to create a much more pleasant experience for himself and those around him.

Like Wyatt, you are in charge of creating your reality. Whatever you focus on becomes your experience. If you focus on the negative aspects of an event, your experience will be negative. The more you focus on the negative aspects, the stronger your negative beliefs will become.

> *COOL FACT: Whether you spend your time and energy focusing on the negatives or the positives of any situation, you will spend your time and energy in some way. Why not focus on the positive aspects, rather than the negatives, and create happy experiences for yourself?*

You deserve to be happy, and you have the power to create happiness for yourself and be an example for others to become happy as well.

Self-Reflection

What is your biggest takeaway from this chapter?

106 | I WOULD, BUT MY DAMN MIND WON'T LET ME!

How can you use what you've just learned to take charge of your mind and be a happier, more confident you?

CHAPTER 8

I'm Not Safe

"**I**'m not safe" can refer to both physical safety and emotional safety and often shows up as:
- "People want to hurt me physically or emotionally."
- "I'm too weak to defend myself."
- "People are evil."
- "People take advantage of me."
- "The world is so scary."

Case Study: Hurtful Hunter
Client: Hunter, Age 14

Presenting Problem

Hunter began seeing his school counselor several weeks ago at his principal's insistence, after yet another fistfight. This was his third fight in two months.

Apparently, Hunter didn't want to see the counselor, but he was told that if he didn't, he would be kicked out of school. Though Hunter reluctantly agreed, he has barely engaged in the sessions because he does not trust the people at school. His mother, Monica, has brought him to the clinic because she is concerned about Hunter's escalating anger and lack of self-control.

Family History

Hunter lives with his mom; his younger brother, Henry; and his maternal grandmother, Betsy. Both parents work outside the home. His father, who no longer lives with the family, has a high-stress job managing road-construction crews. His mother works as a waitress at a local diner, often returning home late at night.

Hunter reports that his parents were always away when he was growing up. Even when they were home, they rarely did much beyond fighting between themselves. The fights would quickly escalate, with his father leaving abruptly and sometimes not coming back for days. Hunter did his best to shield Henry from the fights and would make special efforts to spend time playing with his little brother.

After the divorce three months ago, Hunter, Henry, and Monica moved in with the boys' maternal grandmother in a neighboring town. This past summer was the best time Hunter could remember. Everyone got along well, and for the first time in a long time, his mother seemed relaxed and happy.

Social History

Hunter has always been athletic, excelling at all sports. He used to love participating in after-school sports, but since starting this new school, he has decided instead to devote his time to lifting heavy weights in the gym. Although Hunter's social interest has been steadily declining, his attitude has been generally okay—that is, until this school year.

Within the first few months of school, Hunter got into three fistfights. Hunter reports he was just defending himself. His classmates, however, disagree and say Hunter is a bully, always picking on people.

Words Others Often Use to Describe Hunter

Handsome, charming, thoughtful, helpful, athletic, and, more recently, a bully, mean-spirited, troublemaker

Words Hunter Uses to Describe Himself

Protector, anxious, angry, loner, on edge

Session One Notes

Hunter is well developed physically and appears much older than his age. He is soft-spoken and has a sharp eye for details. He notices every aspect of the décor in the office and enjoys expressing his opinion when things seem out of place.

Hunter doesn't want to be here any more than he wanted to see his school counselor. He has only agreed to come because his mother pleaded with him to give our session a try.

Hunter doesn't want to talk about himself but speaks about Henry openly and with great affection. Hunter says he's like Henry's dad because he has been the one taking care of him. It is Hunter who feeds Henry, reads him bedtime stories, and helps him with his schoolwork, since neither parent is typically available.

Henry is extremely shy and awkward around other people. He rarely talks. When he does, his voice is loud, and he laughs inappropriately. When things get overwhelming for Henry, he usually shuts down, refusing to look at anyone or say anything. Luckily, he attended school with most of his classmates for multiple years, so they learned to leave him alone whenever he was in that state. But that was prior to the recent move.

For most of the session, we continue talking about Henry. Each time the fights are mentioned, Hunter quickly deflects with another amusing Henry story. Before he leaves, Hunter asks for advice on how to help Henry calm down when he's overwhelmed. So, we spend the remaining time discussing a deep-breathing exercise and how to "choose calm." We practice those exercises until Hunter feels confident that he can teach Henry the same.

Session Two Notes

Hunter returns in a great mood. He is thankful for having learned the calming exercises, and he has been surprised and pleased by how quickly he can help Henry get back to calm when he becomes overwhelmed. Hunter even shares that he has used these techniques on himself and that they've worked for him as well.

Hunter seems more trusting in this session, but when asked about the fights again, he immediately goes on the defensive, saying that his counselor thought he was a loser and only wanted to "keep him in line." He didn't want to tell her anything because he was certain it would be used against him. Besides, Hunter feels those fights were justified and that he was doing the right thing. When asked why the fights were justified, Hunter responds he was only protecting Henry. Hunter shares that the kids at the new school were bullying Henry, making fun of him because of his loud voice and inappropriate laughter. Henry's sense of overwhelm got the better of him, and he started crying uncontrollably in front of his classmates, which caused the teasing and bullying to escalate. Hunter shares that it was up to him to protect Henry and to teach those kids a lesson. Even though Hunter feels good that he can stop the bullies, he also shares that he's a little scared of how quickly his anger can escalate, and that he seems to lose control of himself when he's angry.

Following this disclosure, Hunter must feel that he's revealed too much because he promptly clams up again, refusing to share more about the fights or his anger.

We spend the rest of the session discussing various healing modalities. Hunter is fascinated with hypnosis and says he would consider giving it a try in the future.

Sessions Three and Four Notes

Hunter is visibly upset when he comes in today. Apparently, he got into another fistfight earlier and was expelled from school. Hunter says he doesn't care that he was expelled, but he's upset because he hates seeing his mom so worried. Hunter says he's tired of seeing his mom hurt, and he is willing to do what it takes to learn to control himself so that his mom can be happy again.

Even though Hunter wants help, talking about himself is still very uncomfortable for him. After much reassurance that hypnosis is not mind control, Hunter is willing to give it a try.

It takes some time for Hunter to unwind and enter a relaxed state, where he is able to access and talk about his experiences calmly.

The first memory Hunter shares is one of a fight between his parents when Hunter was seven. Hunter recalls that he and Henry were watching TV when suddenly his father started yelling loudly at his mom. Hunter ran into the kitchen and saw his mom crying at the table. Hunter walked over to his mom to comfort her. Before he got there, though, his dad angrily shouted at Hunter to go to his room and mind his own business.

Hunter had not seen his dad this angry before. He didn't know what to do, so he ran out of the room, crying. Hunter remembers being so afraid that his dad would come after him, or even hurt his mom.

For the next few months, the fighting continued and escalated. Hunter wasn't sure what was worse—his dad yelling, his mom pleading for him to stop, or his little brother crying loudly in response. Hunter felt so helpless. He didn't know what to do other than to take his little brother to his room and distract him with TV shows. Hunter felt so ashamed for not doing more, but he was too afraid to approach his dad when he was in one of his moods.

His dad was unpredictable. Sometimes, he would come home in a good mood and would act as if they were the happiest family ever. There would be months where everything was okay, then out of nowhere, his dad would blow up, and the yelling and screaming would go on for hours. Hunter dreaded when his dad came home because he never knew what mood his dad was going to be in.

For the next several years, Hunter and Henry would often sleep in the same bed. Neither one felt safe sleeping alone. Hunter felt like such a coward for being afraid and for being too weak to protect his mom.

During our session, Hunter is surprised by how much shame, guilt, and anger he feels as he recalls those fights, and he can see how they have been affecting him and his decisions. With that awareness, Hunter is now ready to work on releasing his unhelpful emotions.

Root Cause

Hunter reports being pleasantly surprised that he feels significantly better after our last two sessions. He is now ready to discuss things openly.

Hunter recalls the biggest fight he'd ever witnessed between his parents occurred when he was twelve years old. Even though Hunter was terrified of his dad, he couldn't bear hearing his mother's continued crying. He knew his dad was out of control, so he approached him calmly and said, "Dad, you are scaring everyone. Please stop." Before Hunter could say another word, his father pushed him aside and yelled, "You should be scared. You all should be scared. You don't know what I can do to you… to all of you!"

Hunter fell backwards. His mom rushed toward him, but his dad stepped in front of her and demanded that she teach "that boy some manners or else you both will see just how scary I can be." And with that, his dad pushed his mom forcefully into a wall.

Instinctively, Hunter ran toward his mom. Before he could get to her, Hunter's dad grabbed him by the arm and yanked him back towards him. Shaking from fear and anger, Hunter did his best to compose himself and screamed at his dad to "stop hurting Mom!"

Hunter's words came out shrieky, as if he was going through puberty. His dad laughed loudly and demanded, "What are you going to do about it?" and pushed Hunter hard. All the shame and anger Hunter was holding in came rushing out full force as Hunter lunged for his dad. His dad stumbled and fell. Hunter couldn't stop. He flew on top of his dad, punching him with all his might.

Hunter cannot remember much of what happened next. All he recalls is his mom pulling him off his dad and begging him to stop.

Hunter and his dad both stood up slowly. His dad looked over at Hunter and then at his mom, shook his head, backed away, and left. Hunter's mom hugged him tightly, pulling him away just long enough to make sure he was okay.

In that moment, Hunter felt:
    1. Scared: "What did I just do?"

2. Powerful: "I can stand up to my dad and protect my mom."
3. Happy: "Mom is okay, I'm okay, Henry is okay."
4. Safe: "I don't have to be afraid anymore."
5. Shame: "Why did I let this go on for so long?"

Hunter remembers making a promise to himself that from that moment on, he was going to protect his mom and brother no matter what. He was determined to make sure no one would hurt them ever again.

When his dad came home, he acted like nothing had happened, as he had done many times in the past. For months, all was quiet around the house. Hunter was so proud of himself for stepping in and "fixing" his family.

Back in the session, Hunter is shocked by how vivid his recall is, and how he feels all those emotions as intensely now as when they first occurred. Hunter also realizes that he felt these exact emotions each time he got into a fistfight recently. Hunter finally understands the reason why his anger escalated so quickly was because of these pent-up emotions and the promise to himself to keep his loved ones safe.

Hunter doesn't realize that, subconsciously, he developed a program that kicks in whenever he feels powerless—especially in situations where he thinks someone is hurting people he loves. His actions, while violent and problematic, have served as an unhealthy coping mechanism to restore a sense of control for him, helping him feel safe and able to protect his loved ones.

For the next few sessions, we work on releasing his unhelpful emotions and their associated triggers.

Three-Month Follow-Up

Hunter practically shines with happiness when he walks through the office door. With a huge smile on his face, he reports that things at home are great, and that he has started playing basketball again and is getting along well with his teammates. He has been doing the exercises that he learned in our sessions to reprogram his mind, and consequently, he feels much more in control of himself.

As an example, Hunter shares a recent incident with his dad, who got upset because Henry wasn't ready to leave for their weekly visit. Hunter felt the old agitation bubbling up, and his initial instinct was to turn on his aggressions, but instead, he closed his eyes, took a few deep breaths, and clenched and unclenched his fists until he felt calm again. Then, Hunter approached his dad with a smile and said, "All ready, Dad, let's go!" and started asking his dad about his day. His dad smiled back and the three of them headed for the car.

Hunter is so proud of himself for being able to prevent a potential fight. He loves being able to influence his environment positively instead of using physical aggression.

Lesson Learned

What Hunter experienced is a great example of how powerful our mind truly is in its creation of "programs" to keep us "safe."

For so long, Hunter felt unsafe in his house and around his dad. He felt weak, powerless, and ashamed that he couldn't protect his mom. But in that one moment of rage, Hunter reacted with so much force that it got his dad to stop his aggression against him and his mom. At that moment, his subconscious mind created a new belief that for Hunter to stay safe (and protect the people he loves), he had to react with violence. While many subconscious programs to keep us safe are helpful, some can be very unhealthy and actually create more harm and negative outcomes.

In the case of Hunter, whenever he felt that his mother or brother were being mistreated, his mind would be flooded with memories of the fights between his parents and all the powerlessness he'd felt. This would trigger his fight-or-flight response and quickly escalate into physical violence. In the past, Hunter thought the only way to stay safe was to show that he was strong by using violence. Even then, this coping mechanism wasn't aligned with his naturally good nature and ended up causing him much anxiety, making him feel edgy and out of control.

Once Hunter understood the triggers behind his actions and released the unhelpful emotions that fueled them, he was able to pause, bring himself to a calm state, and decide what he would like to do next. This gave Hunter the true power and internal peace he wanted.

COOL FACT: You are the boss of your mind. It is up to you to give your assistant the commands that bring you closer and closer to your goals and dreams.

Self-Reflection

What is your biggest takeaway from this chapter?

_____
_____
_____
_____
_____
_____
_____
_____
_____
_____
_____
_____
_____
_____
_____
_____
_____
_____
_____
_____

How can you use what you've just learned to take charge of your mind and be a happier, more confident you?

_____
_____
_____
_____
_____
_____
_____
_____
_____
_____
_____
_____
_____
_____
_____
_____
_____
_____
_____
_____
_____
_____
_____
_____
_____
_____

A Powerful Beginning

Congratulations on reading this book. We're sure you have gained knowledge and insight into your mind and understand how to control your thoughts, emotions, and actions more effectively. But this is not just the end of a book, it's a new beginning for you!

You now know that all your thoughts and feelings are commands to your mind. Those thoughts and feelings determine what is placed into your IC, and your experience of life is shaped by that. You also know that YOU are in control of your thoughts, and YOU get to determine what each life experience means to you. YOU get to set your mood and choose your response to whatever is happening around you!

Yes, you have so much more control than you realized and now you have tips and tools to practice that control. Over time, with deliberate focus, you will become a master of creating your reality. We've even produced a companion workbook with step-by-step guidance to make daily practice of these new skills simple for even faster results. Whatever goals and dreams you have will be reached and accomplished with much more ease than you have ever imagined!

If you find yourself feeling unhappy about your situation, pause, re-evaluate, and redecide on a course of action that best serves your needs. Use powerful, positive self-talk that programs your mind for happiness and success. Catch yourself when negative self-talk creeps in and quickly correct your programming commands. You can do this as often as you want!

Thousands of teens are living in quiet desperation right now because they have not been taught how to use their mind as the key to success in life. Our goal in writing this book is to illustrate for you the power of your mind so you can take control of your thoughts, feelings, and actions. You are in charge of creating the life that you want and deserve.

You deserve to be successful and happy. You now have the knowledge and the power to make it happen!

About the Authors

Jacqui Letran and Joseph Wolfgram are a husband-and-wife team with a passion for helping people live their best through education, healing, and good mental health.

Jacqui Letran is a Multi-Award-Winning Author, Nurse Practitioner, and Teen Confidence Expert with over twenty years of experience guiding youth to optimal physical and mental health.

Twelve years ago, Jacqui left her private medical clinics to start a holistic healing practice to help teens discover their authentic voice, own their self-worth, and be the best, healthiest version of themselves.

Drawing from her extensive experience helping thousands of clients heal from their mental and emotional struggles, Jacqui writes easy-to-understand books that help teens create unshakable self-esteem, self-confidence, and self-love.

Joseph Wolfgram holds degrees in Psychology and Business Administration and is retired from the IT (Information Technology) industry as a healthcare CTO (Chief Technology Officer). He is master-certified as a Practitioner in Neuro Linguistic Programming (NLP), a Hypnotherapist (MCHt), and an Executive Coach.

An accomplished Speaker, Joseph presents at industry conferences, expert panel discussions, and mentoring workshops focused on advancing women in technology. Joseph is co-host of Stop the Bully Within podcast in support of his desire to see all people achieve their greatest potential.

With Gratitude

We would like to express to our family, clients, teachers, and mentors (whether in a professional relationship or in life) a heartfelt thank you for being a part of our lives. Your presence has helped us grow and transform and now we are able to give back in the form of this book.

To our children Alan Letran, Joe Wolfgram, and Ayla Wolfgram, thank you for being our biggest life teachers and sources of endless joy.

To our editor, Laura Martone, thank you so much for your professionalism and expert advice. You are a joy to work with.

Last, but not least, a huge thank you to our amazing beta readers: Margaret Holt-Crerar, Danielle Autry, Crystal Franke McQueary, Tori Wilds Wyckoff, Christine Kozlik, Zen Kozlik, Peggy Shafer, and Iliana Neman. We truly appreciate you all. Your feedback is invaluable and has made this book even more applicable and enjoyable for readers.

Connect with Us

We love hearing from our readers. Please feel free to connect with us at:

www.JacquiLetran.com

Facebook.com/JacquiLetran

Linkedin.com/in/JacquiLetran

Instagram.com/JacquiLetran

You can also contact us at:

Author@JacquiLetran.com

*Thank you so much for reading.
If you enjoyed this book, please consider leaving an honest review via your favorite online store. It would help other readers discover this book as well.*

Thank you in advance!

Jacqui & Joseph

Words of Wisdom for Teens Series
Award-Winning Guides for Teen Girls
(YOUNG MEN VERSION COMING SOON)

5 Simple Steps to Manage Your Mood
A Guide for Teen Girls: How to Let Go of Negative Feelings and Create a Happy Relationship with Yourself and Others

I Would, but MY DAMN MIND Won't Let Me!
A Guide for Teen Girls: How to Understand and Control Your Thoughts and Feelings

Jump-Start Your Confidence and Boost Your Self-Esteem
A Guide for Teen Girls: Unleash Your Inner Superpowers to Conquer Fear and Self-Doubt and Build Unshakable Confidence

Companion Journals

5 Simple Steps to Manage Your Mood
A Companion Journal to Help You Track, Understand, and Take Charge of Your Mood and Create a Happy Relationship with Yourself and Others

I Would, but MY DAMN MIND Won't Let Me!
A Companion Journal to Help You Transform Your Inner Mean Girl into Your Bestie

Jump-Start Your Confidence and Boost Your Self-Esteem
A Companion Journal to Help You Create a Positive and Powerful Mindset to Conquer Anxiety, Fear, and Self-Doubt

Stop the Bully Within Podcast

After seeing thousands of clients, Jacqui noticed a common theme among most of those she's helped—they are their own biggest bully.

Just pause for a moment and think of the words you've said to yourself whenever you did something wrong or failed at something. Are those loving and supportive words? Would you say those same words to someone you love?

For many people, when they think of a bully, they think of someone outside of them—someone who says and does mean things to cause others pain. Not too many people think about the bully they have within themselves.

Jacqui and her husband, Joseph, are on a mission to bring awareness to how damaging this "bully within" can be, and to help people learn how to transform that inner critic into their best friend, cheerleader, and personal champion for success. If this notion resonates with you, please check out the Stop the Bully Within podcast, which Jacqui and Joseph co-host together.

**Listen to the podcast at
https://www.JacquiLetran.com/Podcast**

Made in the USA
Monee, IL
16 September 2024